HORSES *of the* WORLD

Horses *of the* World

From the Desert to the Racetrack

Jacqueline Ripart

Translated from the French by
Molly Stevens and Catherine Reep

Harry N. Abrams, Inc., Publishers

Contents

Introduction — 7

Forgotten Horses of the Namib Desert — 10
NAMIBIA
Since World War I, an unusual herd of horses has been
living wild in the utter hostility of the Namib Desert.

The Sons of the Steppes — 32
MONGOLIA
As the noble heirs of Genghis Khan, cavaliers, archers,
and fighters celebrate the Mongolian horse during the
annual Naadam holiday.

Rumblings and *Fantasias* — 50
THE MAGHREB
The *fantasia* is the living memory of the Maghreb cavaliers.
Burnooses, turbans, and manes in the wind, they come together
for every *moussem* and every national or family holiday.

The Cavaliers of Eternal Japan — 72
JAPAN
Preserving the art of *yabusame*, which was practiced by the
samurai, Japanese archers challenge each other in skill
during equestrian jousts that are sacred in character.

The Dancers of Andalusia — 90
SPAIN
Turning their backs on changing times, the Andalusians
continue to perpetuate traditions that display the
Spanish horse in all of its splendor.

The Last *Cimarrones* — 110
COLOMBIA—VENEZUELA
Although the Wayuus live for the most part off their
livestock, the horse has remained in their eyes the sole
symbol of wealth, prestige, and power.

The Princes of Vienna — 128
AUSTRIA—SLOVENIA
For four centuries, the Spanish Riding School of Vienna has
perpetuated the art of classical riding. Its white stallions,
bred in Lipizza, are admired worldwide.

Birthplace of Stars   148
IRELAND
Known for its mild climate and rich soil, the county of
Kildare is home to some of the most prestigious
stud farms in the world.

The Cowboys of the Twenty-First Century   168
CANADA
Distant cousins to the mythical adventurers of the
Hollywood western, the cowboys of the Canadian West
are skilled riders who combine tradition and progress.

The Steeds of the Sahara   190
TUNISIA
Upholding the tradition of ancient nomads, the horses of
the Sahara are today's racing stars in Tunisia, where nearly
four hundred races take place each year.

The Inhabitants of the Pampas   210
ARGENTINA
In the heart of the Pampas, the criollo horse is more than an
international polo star. He is man's brother, his double:
without him, the gaucho wouldn't exist.

The World of the Trotter   230
FRANCE
Trotting races still bear the stamp of their rural and popular
origins. Trained by a driver who is often its owner, the
trotter is the horse of a single man.

Step by Step in the Andes   248
SOUTH AMERICA
An inseparable companion in work and travel, the paso fino
is also prized for its dancing gait. Horse shows are a part of life.

Introduction

Tell me the horse of a population, I'll tell you about its customs and institutions.

GEORGES CUVIER
French zoologist and paleontologist (1769–1832)

Six thousand years! Six thousand years and much more of a global adventure in which the horse—the cart horse or war horse, the hunting horse or racehorse, for sport or pleasure—has filled the soul of civilizations and cultures throughout the world. A special destiny shaped by its energy and amazing beauty as much as its pride and submission. "The horse is unlike all other animals," Jean Chevalier and Alain Gheerbrant have written in their *Dictionary of Symbols*, "The horse is the mount, the vehicle, the vessel, and its destiny is therefore linked to that of Man." No other animal has lived so close to the human being, no other animal has captivated him for so long. Their relationship, propelled by the most extraordinary dreams, is perpetually being invented.

In the Tertiary period, its ancestor, the vulnerable *Eohippus* that galloped in the forests of North America, was no larger than a fox, but its decline brought about its total extinction, about ten thousand years ago. Their descendants, in the meantime, left their American birthplace, and migrated through the frozen lands of today's Bering Strait to the vast plains of the Old World. Several million years later, the ancestor to today's horses was still only common game hunted by Cro-Magnon man. It would not take much for it to disappear completely from the surface of the earth, for, at the dawn of history, it was only present in the huge steppes of Eurasia. Hence, these are the origins of the first horse of history, of the first horses and the first riders.

The horse very quickly became the invaluable mount of nomadic populations, which erupted from central Asia into all corners of Eurasia. Through invasions and conquests, there was a genuine horse saga during the second millennium that changed the face of the ancient world. Little by little, *Equus caballus* found a home all around the world. Through selection and breeding, people created the diverse races of horses.

Henceforth, this "prince" that became man's handsome "subject" would fill the human imagination with remarkable consistency. With the world on its back, the horse would carry the most fantastic dreams of man, playing a key role in the innumerable myths, tales, and legends of all nations.

This is how it was introduced into the history of Islam: "When Mohammed became a glorious conqueror, he was offered a fiery steed that carried him to the peak of his spiritual mission. His followers explain that, on his miraculous horse Borak, he galloped into the holy night, accompanied by Gabriel, the archangel, from Mecca to the Temple of Jerusalem, and from there he rose to the sky."

The horse has always been the animal that man has used to impressively prove his superiority. It has accompanied the warrior, sharing his glory days until death. In honor of the deceased, the Asian sculptor learned to render the horse, lending it a cosmic dimension: "The dawn is his head, the Sun, his eye, the wind, his breath. The celestial vault is his back . . . when he dies, he thunders."

The memory of small, muscular, and powerful horses, of invaders, already dates far back. Since the Carolingian era, in the west, breeders have been selecting stronger, larger races, to create beasts of burden, draft animals, and warhorses. *Equus caballus* was to become the noble animal of the Middle Ages. Because the horse was a partner in battle and a friend of the cavalier, it was lavishly decorated. But the perfection of its movements was not deemed very important.

Later, the savagery of these battles subsided and was replaced by ceremonial parades, with tunes that directly stemmed from the exercises the knights had to undergo in order to prepare for battle: *levade, piaffe, curvet.* . . . Down to the smallest detail, the art of equitation, which was perfected in 1532 in Naples, continues to strive toward beauty and harmony.

In 1494, Christopher Columbus landed on the island of Hispaniola (present-day Haiti), with 34 Andalusian stallions and brood mares, America had not yet met this noble horse. But, in less than a hundred years, the conquistadors scattered their breeds over the entire continent, and the horse became part of Indian religion, cults, war, and the household. Meanwhile, in the vast plains that were conquered by Europeans, there emerged a rider by vocation: the cowboy.

In the Old World, when urban civilization had already begun pushing back the countryside and when agriculture had begun to eat away at forests, the horse played a major role in society. It became the emblem of prestige throughout the large royal and courtly stables, and later the emblem of fashionable and popular society horse events. The horse was also at the root of specific professions. In fact, horse racing was eventually welcomed with boundless enthusiasm, especially in the country from which the railroad came: England.

The career of horses in the military ended with World War II. The age of mounted cavaliers was over for good. The horse surrendered quickly, for it was surely never as warlike and heroic as the poets liked to claim!

In this new millennium, the love we have for horses seems like the very model of this bond expressed through history. In the five continents, natural, instinctive, spontaneous, and popular horseback riding coexists with the world of formal riding techniques, schools, academies, riders, and masters. Nevertheless, the picture of a wild stallion continues to fascinate us. It's almost universal.

To set out to meet the horses of the world, and the cultures and arts that involve them; to discover the many faces, the humblest of which are just as moving; that is the goal of this book.

Forgotten Horses of the Namib Desert

NAMIBIA

It is the strangest herd in the world. These horses learned to survive
in the utter hostility of the Namib Desert, almost without grass,
and often without water. Fierce.

History

In 1870, Thomas Henry Huxley, one of the most brilliant champions of Darwin, set out to trace the evolutionary adventure of the horse since its emergence, which dates back some fifty-five million years. He used three fossils found in Europe as a starting point. Soon, however, he had to consider the discoveries of a certain Othniel C. Marsh, the leading expert in the paleontology of vertebrates. Sure enough, the latter presented him with a series of horse fossils that he uncovered out in the western United States, proving that the history of the horse began in America, and that the European fossils belonged to three distinct migrations of American stock.

The two studies conducted by these specialists yielded the first illustration of the evolution of the horse, one of the most famous in the history of science: a decreasing number of toes, a steady growth in molar length, and an evolution of body and size, from 14 inches, forty million years ago, to more than 4 feet in height (12 to 14 hands). These transformations point to the adaptation to environmental changes that forced the Eohippus, the "dawn horse," to leave its forest home to live in the plains. Fifteen million years ago, as many as nineteen species in the horse family are believed to have lived in an isolated North America. But their decline brought about their total extinction, about ten thousand years ago. Their descendants, in the meantime, left their American birthplace, migrating through the frozen lands of today's Bering Strait to the vast plains of the Old World, constituting a new genealogical tree of many branches. All became extinct in this case too, except for one, named *Equus*, composed of seven species: three asses, four donkeys and onagers, and the *Equus caballus*, the horse.

The first signs of horse domestication were found in the south of Ukraine, at Dereivka, and date back to six thousand years ago. This is late in comparison to dog, cattle, sheep, and pig domestication. But the practice of horse domestication grew quickly, and was successful worldwide. The horse was formed, refined,

A horse is worth more than riches.

SPANISH PROVERB

and perfected through selection and crossbreeding through the ages, through every civilization, in accordance with the practice of equitation and other forms of use. But what happened to the last wild survivors of the *Equus caballus* species?

The Tarpan horse, which lived in herds in the plains of eastern Europe, was exterminated by the peasants, who accused them of destroying the harvests and of stealing the domestic mares. The last Tarpan seems to have been destroyed around 1880. The last wild horse, which lived in Central Asia, was the Przewalski, named for the Russian officer and explorer who had observed the horses in 1876 in Mongolia. This species too was hunted down, but it survives in captivity, and a few Przewalskis have been reintroduced to the wild in Mongolia.

Can we say that the Przewalski is the only wild horse in our times? If we take the adjective "wild" in its etymological sense, that is "not tamed," the answer is no. Indeed, in the uninhabited regions of the steppes and desert, some horses that have fled their masters or escaped a battle have bred as feral animals and have survived in the wild. Today, there are some thirty thousand Mustangs in the United States, almost six hundred thousand brumbies in Australia, a few dozen horses in the Namib Desert and on deserted islands off the American continent. But all of them come from domestic horses that have gone back to living on their own. And, in the eyes of biologists, this is an important distinction, since appearance and genetic knowledge differ.

Nevertheless, free horses are in a precarious situation, and their future is uncertain. Deemed useless, of no economic value, and taking up land that could be better used, they are now threatened. "Wild" or "gone wild," they nevertheless represent a precious heritage.

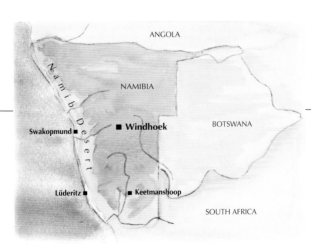

Their silhouettes and even their movements reveal the characteristics of their forefathers who were imported from Germany, England, and South Africa at the end of the nineteenth century. But they all bear the grace and nobility of the purebred Arabian, the common ancestor to most equine races.

Two oceans touch each other. Edge to edge, waves and dunes. Separated by a thin border of foam, joined together every morning by a thick curtain of fog. Water and sand move in the same way in the wind. There, in the wake of the Benguela current, the icy tides of the Atlantic Ocean swarm with life. Here, beneath the burning breath of a molten sun, the earth seems to have been emptied out. This is the Namib Desert.

Namib, in African *Nama*, is the "country where there is nothing." It is the oldest desert on the planet.

In midsummer, temperatures climb to 158°F on the ground. During winter nights, they drop to 5°C below zero. As soon as day breaks, all life wastes away under a sun that chars both sand and rock. Except for a few of the oddest creatures. For example, the little Coleoptera beetle, which, every morning, folds its legs in front, extends its back legs, and waits, its head beneath, for the fog to condense on its elytra and form a drop of water, which it brings to its mouth. The oryx, massive gazelles, have a brain equipped with a vein network that is special enough to withstand the hottest temperatures. In order to survive, moles, springboks, ostriches, lizards, and birds have developed equally extraordinary anatomical tactics. But horses, in the land of unbearable Nothingness? They have been surviving in a small part of the desert ever since they were abandoned by the cavalrymen of the German imperial army that was battling with South Africa during World War I. Access to

PREVIOUS PAGE: *With the first rain of austral spring, the pastures turn green again. Horses take advantage of the ponds that are quickly dried out by the harsh sun.*

The survival of this wild herd depends on reproduction. Therefore, the mares protect their colts and the stallions defend their harem. A stop at the watering place is a time for rest, relaxation, play, and maternal tenderness.

They live in herds out of the simple pleasure of being together and manage to feel very close.

BUFFON, GEORGES LOUIS LECLERC,
Comte de Buffon
French naturalist (1707–1788)
Citation from the book *Histoire Naturelle*

A few drops of rain are all that are needed to fill rock crevices along the sand's surface. Horses twist into all kinds of positions in order to reach the bottom of these short-lived drinking spots.

this area has been strictly forbidden since diamonds were discovered in 1908. In this camel-colored expanse, the sands foam into waves, crescents, stars. Only the treaded ground around a watering point indicates the unexpected presence of horses.

They arrive as soon as day breaks. The shadows of the night draw away from them. Here they are! A family quickly trots across the immense sand plain. In the round frame of binoculars, their silhouette is tousled, sculpted by the wind of galloping and the strength of the sun. Strong, shining muscles that flex as they work; long tangled horsehair. A rowdy gallop. A few feet from the water, they suddenly stop short. They have reached their goal.

Other horses appear from all directions. There are now more than thirty that have come to quench their thirst. They push and shove. The dominant males round up their mares and show their teeth to their rivals. A curious young horse has come too close. With a haughty air and cunning neck, the head of the family charges, bucking and rearing. The young bachelor is not even three years old. He pulls away, head lowered, a sign of surrender. The incident is over.

A cry can be heard amidst the neighing. A chestnut colt with white stockings teeters and turns desperately. Its mother comes and presses against it. Her feet planted in the sand, her head held high, she offers her teats.

The white light crushes colors and flattens surfaces. And so all the horses seem to have the same bay coat. To tell them apart, you have to distinguish their age and sex, detect the particularities of their coats, the tufts on their necks or the scars on their body, and observe their behavior. Their

*Movement is the original element of this being,
a joyful movement in spaces where they are free.*

HANS HEINRICH ISENHART

social structure is that of all free horses: a dominant male surrounded by its harem of mares and their colts, no more than a dozen or so. The mares are very loyal and the families are stable. But the ruthless laws of the hierarchy exclude the young male from his original family as soon as he is two years old. From that point on, he lives alone before joining a group of bachelors. Submitting to the dominant male, he will then learn to behave appropriately through power struggles, and he will prepare himself for a family of his own.

Every year, in mating season, with the first rains of the southern spring, this is how the young male tries his luck: to steal a filly for his family, he declares a merciless war against the leader, who will sometimes fight to the point of death to protect his harem.

The worst enemy of these horses, however, is drought. Records successively show a major fluctuation in the population of these desert horses: They were thought to number three hundred in 1983, sixty-five in 1984, and two hundred seventy-six in 1991, the first year of the systematic census. Two years later, in hopes of preventing too much grazing, the Namibian authorities decided to capture about one hundred of them. The family groups were shattered and by the end of the dry season there were only one hundred seventeen. But the males and mares that survived found the strength to reproduce. As long as this horse population doesn't exceed one hundred fifty, there will be no more horses captured by the government. According to Namibian experts, this part of the desert cannot accommodate more because of its fragile ecosystem.

The size of the horses seems magnified when, from afar,

you see their slender silhouettes in this barren landscape. Yet the most robust in the herd measure 15 hands at the most. These horses are so well adapted to the desert that, despite the heat, dry wind, and absence of grass, they can go without water for several days straight, while traveling across their nearly 99,000 acres. This territory is wedged between the high, impenetrable dunes and the high Namibian plateau, which is used to breed livestock. It's a territory the horses will never leave.

They are prisoners of this watering place, the only one in the region. Moreover, their history coincides with it, as the archives of the Namibian Ministry for the Protection of Nature proves.

Baron von Wolf, *Herr Baron*, officer of William II, a man of tradition, of great fortune; and a man of horses, acquired the Duwisib farm and its more than 123,000 acres of land, in the Namib desert, in 1907. Even before his "neo-romantic" castle was finished, he had stallions and brood mares sent by train from South Africa. They were crossbred with English and Arabian purebreds and German half-breeds that were crossed locally, with the blood of the Quagga, the small wild horse family that is now extinct.

Obsessed with improving his breeding, the Baron later imported several Hanover, Trakehners, and Hackney horses by boat from Germany and England. He regularly covered some of his mares with the stallions of the German imperial stud farm of Nauchas, near Windhoek, the Namibian capital. What follows is a letter that he wrote to the head of the institution:

Dear Baron König,
I am sending you the following mares. . . . Please pay special attention to Good Night, a broodmare with a chestnut coat, her sire being Bonito by Satanella, who suffers from a foot problem, and requires special care. . . .

This information explains the lameness that many of the wild herd have today, affected by a congenital hoof deformity. In a photo album dating back to 1912, the descriptions that accompany the pictures note coats, origins, and lineage, including that of the famous English Thoroughbred Crackerjack.

Other memories: In 1908, the Germans built a railroad between Namibia and South Africa. During its construction,

The horse is the king of speed; it is the fastest of the quadrupeds: it outruns the stag, leaps like the roe deer and tires the wolf. Quicker than the wind, filled with more rage than mountain torrents, it yields only to the hurricane.

HEPHREM HOUEL
Director of National Stud Farms
in France (1807–1885)

Fighting can involve bucking and biting and is an attempt to establish supremacy over the group; but there is also play and affection.

LEFT: *The young male is excluded from his original family as early as age two. He then joins a group of bachelors and learns how to fight, hold his rank, and prepare to found a harem.*

In the midst of this silent and tormented sea, life surprisingly triumphs: plants can store mist, trees draw what they need to survive from layers of water underground, insects drink fog, and, wonder of wonders, the rain invents its instantaneous spring. The desert is suddenly green with thousands of small shoots, the horses dance on the still damp orange sand . . .

In the distance, the dunes, draped in a carmine veil, blend into the night. A rumble rises. It's the unkempt and aggressive herd approaching, fiercer than the German cavalrymen and as blazing as the harsh desert sun.

The Sons of the Steppes

MONGOLIA

They sleep in the white and round *ger*—the felt tents that have been part of life for thousands of years—, gallop across the vast plain, revere their children thrown on war-horses. Cavalrymen, archers and fighters, these are the sons of Genghis Khan.

Once he domesticated the horse, man heaved himself on its back. The first images of mounted horses are Babylonian, and date back to about four thousand years ago. But riding was not documented until about 1360 B.C.E. The oldest treatise on the maintenance and training of warhorses was found in the ruins of the city of Hattusas, some eighty miles outside of Ankara. It is an unusual text, written in Hittite and engraved in cuneiform characters on clay tablets, attributed to a master horseman named Kikkuli.

At the dawn of historic time, and all through the second millennium B.C.E., the Achaeans, the Mitanni people, the Hyksos, the Hittites, the Medes, the Persians, Scythians, and Parthians had headed toward the west. The use of cavalry soon moved to North Africa, Central Asia, and Greece. During the fourth century B.C.E., the first mounted riders poured into the Roman West, spreading word of an unknown world. The Goths and the Huns hauled the fruits of a civilization for which the Scythians provided

for more than a millennium B.C.E. A civilization that owes a lot—if not everything—to the horse, the king of the steppes. The equestrian qualities that these people had were also shared by their neighbors in Asia, the Buryats, the Yakuts, the Tungus, and the Kalmucks, who eventually began moving as well. The great nomads of Eurasia all had a passion for horses, not to say their cult, a shared collection of beliefs, or the same techniques which they spread to others. In the meantime, inventions were coming out of Asia, such as the saddle and stirrups, and being refined in the West.

The most amazing saga in history was that of the stream of Mongolians, an entire population that terrorized a large part of humanity in the thirteenth century as they migrated. The fierce warriors of Genghis Khan set out in groups of a thousand and more, clinging on their small and powerful horses, the descendants of the Przewalski horses that had been living in the steppes for thousands of years. These horses were certainly not as elegant as

Man, surrounded by elements that concocted his ruin, by animals with speed and strength greater than his own, man was once a slave on earth; the horse made him king.

HEPHREM HOUEL

Arabians, nor were they as strong as the European steeds, but their endurance was unmatched, and their rustic character was one of the major assets of the Great Khan's armies.

It is perhaps the cruel harshness of their native land that is at the origin of Mongolian expansion. The steppe region is indeed a land of extremes, a territory forever being swept by winds. Snow swirls through the area all through the winter and the blazing summer sun burns the thin pastures. Closely bonded to each other, man and horse gallop away, propelled by the pressing need for a better life. Genghis Khan was among them. Born with the name Temujin, in 1167, among a tribe living to the north of the Gobi Desert, he first subjugated his neighbors before naming himself khan at age twenty. Then he set out to subjugate the tribes of the steppes of Asia and thus unified all the Mongolian peoples. From that moment on, he conquered an immense empire that was to last until the fifteenth century.

The Great Khan's genius was linked to the use of his great army of cavalrymen, which they say included up to 250,000 men divided into several groups. Their mobility was unmatched. Born hunters, they waged war in the same way they hunted, with great pleasure. The cavalrymen, armed with axes, sabers, lances, and lassos, made up the "clash-and-conquer" strength. The archers, protected by leather, led the mobile attacks against the enemies. This military strategy proved its superiority over the western system, which was based on battle lines and cavalry charges.

In less than eleven years, and at the cost of incredible massacres, Genghis Khan built the largest empire of all time, from the Pacific Ocean to the Caspian Sea and from the Amur River to the Volga. This is the amazing work of a man who was to immortalize this old land, the home of the wind and the first cavaliers.

RUSSIA

Altai Mongol

Altai de Gobi

Ulan-Bator

MONGOLIA

Gobi Desert

Inner Mongolia

CHINA

*As soon as the Soviet Empire fell,
the Mongolians quickly restored
honor to their traditions and the
cult of their great ancestor,
Genghis Khan. They returned
to their nomadic lives on which
they depend for survival.*

There is nothing like the
Mongolian steppe. The horizon looks as if the blue sky
were cut with a saber. Gray, green, and brown grass
stretches out everywhere and into the distance. There
are no hedges or tall trees to stop the Arctic winds. The
immense steppe, worn like old felt, seems to drift with the
light. A Mongolian's heritage is the back of his war-horse,
his home is his tent. His religion and his legends speak only
of the horse. No one travels by foot, not prince or the elderly,
not women or children. Everyone lives in a saddle.

Mongolia: hardly more than two million inhabitants for
a livestock of thirty million—sheep, cattle, goats, and
camels—including three million horses, direct descendants
of the primitive Tarpan or Przewalski horse. Free on their
land of origin, they live its barrenness, its freezing nights
and torments, with silent and patient resignation. The
Mongolians do very little breaking, a kind of "minimal
domestication." It's a matter for men, for the horses won't
allow people to approach them, and it's even more difficult
to catch them. As soon as they are trained to wear a saddle,
they are nevertheless amazingly obedient. And children
learn to ride them before they learn to walk.

Of course, the Mongolian horse does not match the
standards of the "civilized" horse: 14 hands tall, a short
neck, massive, a thick head, etc. But its vigor, power, and
endurance stand the test of time. "Genghis Khan was the
master of the world; the master of Genghis Khan was his

horse," wrote Paul Morand in his *Histoire de Chevaux* [History
of Horses]. Genghis Khan: the most illustrious of Mongolian
leaders, who, in the thirteenth century, built the largest
empire of all time with his "great army" of cavalrymen. But
Genghis Khan, who was so venerated by the people of the
steppe, was banished by the Supreme Soviet. Even his
name became taboo. There was neither a street nor a statue
to commemorate him, only a few words in school textbooks
denouncing his "imperialism." The Mongolians, freed from
their Communist yoke in 1991, quickly restored honor to the
cult of their great ancestor, and also to the horse.

The Tsagaan Sar race, which takes place during the full
moon of the new year, is being celebrated again. It is the fes-
tivity that the cavalrymen of the "omnipotent king" preferred, and it included a real horse race and genuine betting.
Every July 11, the famous Naadam national holiday is celebrated in the eighteen provinces known as *aïmaks*.

A few days before the start of the festivities, several
thousand nomads head towards Ulan Bator, the capital.
People arrive on horseback, with children, herds, and
chariots overflowing with beds, drums, painted trunks, and
felt and cord rugs, just as in the times of the Great Khan,
when they would go to town on the days of the fair.
Between wrestling matches and archery competitions, the
top horses go head to head in a seven to fifteen-mile race.
The jockeys, both girls and boys, are featherweights between the ages of five and twelve. They all join the celebration, because a victory would catapult them into adulthood.
And also because, whenever the care of a horse is involved, a
Mongolian is happy. Sedip, white cap on two high cheek-

At a very young age, children learn to respect and love horses. They quickly learn to ride them, break them in, and distinguish the best steeds.

Mongolian horses are raised in the wild in the steppes. There is a rodeo at age two, when they are broken in. To capture them, riders use the urgha, *a lasso attached to the end of a long pole.*

Sheep, goats, and oxen live near the camp. Women and children watch over them and fence them in at night.

An honorable man has only one word.
And honorable horse has only one gait.

MONGOLIAN PROVERB

bones, is among them. He has already learned to break horses, to pick out the best among them. He always has a single goal in mind: the Naadam race. This year, he dreams of winning the 15-mile race. He is ten years old and hungry for glory. Accompanied by his family, he has been riding for four days to reach the outskirts of the capital.

The white *ger*—the felt tents that have been part of the life since time immemorial—sprout up everywhere on the soft grass. Nomads camp. The horses are tied down, their heads hang as they falter from tuft to tuft. Men and women with their forever smiling wrinkles tend to their business quietly. The wild eyes of the horses. The smooth faces of the young riders. Near a brook from which the horses take turns drinking, Tömöriyn, Sedip's trainer, makes final adjustments on the saddles. He too came from the region known as Gobi-Altaï. He traveled almost 100 miles with his family, moving from pasture to pasture, from lake to the tall sand dunes, following a specific route. His summer camping site, at the northernmost end, brings him closer ever year to Ulan Bator. There, for almost three years, Tömöriyn has been preparing his horse, a seven-year-old gelding—the Mongolians don't ride mares or stallions—that was worked to lose its "bad fat." At present, the animal's sweat ìs no longer "dirty," no longer "greasy." He says that it is "damp." The horse is all set. The race is full of promise.

Daybreak is icy. The sun, to the east, balances on the edge of the world. A peppery smell of artemisia rises from the treaded ground of the steppes. They have already set out on horse-back, entire families wearing heavy boots with toes pointing upward, a *deel* of crimson, antique gold, wine, or ultramarine blue with yellow around it, and a felt hat on the head.

In the steppes, horse racing brings together owners and fans by the thousands. All the jockeys are children. Because of their light weight, their mount can gallop over long distances.

FOLLOWING SPREAD: *Running at top speed for the final sprint, after about twenty miles of terrain, the little riders of the Naadam gallop towards the finish line before a wild crowd.*

A short speech opens the Naadam. It's followed by a "long chant," which rises straight up like the smoke from an autumn fire. A parade, an official procession, fanfare. Then, over the loud speaker, two races and the first rounds of wrestling are announced. The young jockeys, their faces round like the moon, their eyes filled with innocence, head one at a time to the starting point, 15 miles away. No whips are used, only rope. And there are songs to cheer on the mounts, distant echoes of Tibetan prayers passed down by their ancestors. They are standing straight up on their stirrups.

In the nearby stadium, the wrestling fans are ready to burst. Four referees have taken their places. The competitors arrive two at a time, puffing up their chests, their satin shorts shimmering red and blue, wearing boleros with tailored arms. The "eagle fight" can begin. The goal is to bring your adversary's shoulders to the ground, or only the head, elbow, or knee. They bound like a bird of prey, their arms like wings. It's a noble and slow sport. It isn't violent, only strength wins. The winner dons the victory headpiece

and opens his arms wide. Meanwhile, the defeated contestant can only walk like an everyday mortal.

Suddenly, a secret, almost inaudible rumbling comes from the landscape. The crowd stirs. The trainers, all on horseback, look through binoculars and stand as still as statues. They will be judged while sculpted in a piece of land. They stare. Now, dust clouds the horizon. An echo of hooves beat on the hot ground. A horde of riders charge toward the crowd, lashing the air with their cries. There they are! They all share the fury of victory and the same certitude. A final push and Sedip, who continues to whip his small mount with fuming nostrils, is the first to cross the finish line.

There are cavaliers and animals everywhere. In the middle of this dense crowd, escorted by Tömöriyn, Sedip shines. He won't leave his mount the whole afternoon. One by one, they come to pat the small gelding's neck. *Aïrak* (fermented mare's milk) is poured onto his mane and croup as an offering to the gods. For the victory belongs more to the horse than to the rider. And it is really the trainer who has been successful. His reputation will grow throughout the steppes.

The courage of the Mongolians
Is as infinite as
the quality of their horses
is immense and boundless.

FROM THE SONG *The Mongolian Horse*

Several hundred riders participate
in the big race of the Naadam
every year. Less than half of
them reach the finish line. But
they all celebrate!

The achievements of the day's heroes are celebrated in the *ger* late into the night. Many guests enter unnoticed. They bend down when coming in, then join the men seated on small painted stools around a low table. The sounds from outside are muffled. There is nothing but warmth, color, and merriment. The flames of the oil lamps flicker. To the nomad, the round tent is an essential world center with a horizon as its circumference. It is a hospitable and generous world. There are congratulations, there is praise for the horses, their ancestors, trainers, and riders.

The snuff boxes, decorated with semiprecious stones, are passed around, and everyone breathes in the bitter powder. Then, between two large bowls of *aïrak*, there is concern about the herd, about the vigor of the stallions, and the health of the family. In the background, in the shadows, women and children sit on their beds or rugs. Pastoral tradition is such that it separates the world of women from the world of men. It is the women who are to take care of household chores and raising the children. It is also the women who milk the mares. During the summer each produces three to five quarts of milk a day. This is the time to make cheese, creams,

Returning to the bivouac, families escort the heroes of the day. Their accomplishments will be celebrated under the tents, late into the night.

and butters, and also the *aïrak*, a sparkling beverage with between three and eight percent alcohol. It's considered to be a true elixir of life.

Young girls serve the tea, meat soup, and noodles, the boiled lamb . . . their eyes shine with happiness. A joyful gathering comes and goes. It will be a long and lively night. For the race is always the occasion to offer chants, drunkenness, and joy to the master of Nature. The Mongolians have created their own way of singing to the sky and wine, to tell about the forces that fill the earth, water and clouds Their daily lives are stripped of extravagance.

The feast is always sprinkled with fermented mare's milk, the most loved and most popular drink. Sparkling and refreshing, it is said to also have energetic and therapeutic properties. It is custom for the guest to be served three times, after which he is permitted to serve himself, with as much as he desires.

When the horse is quiet
It is because his master has gone by foot.

MONGOLIAN PROVERB

Rumblings and *Fantasias*

THE MAGHREB

Burnooses, turbans, and manes in the wind, the riders and horses of the Maghreb region of North Africa come together for every *moussem*, every national or family holiday. A history of age-old love between man and his most noble conquest.

The time when the horse arrived in Africa is as imprecise as the men who led them. But the discovery of cave paintings in the Sahara has suggested to historians that horses and chariots appeared around 2000 B.C.E. Are these the horses that were imported into the Libyan ports by the Sea People, whom the Egyptians had repressed? Or did they come by land instead, from the northern shores of the Mediterranean, passing through the fertile land of the Nile Delta? In both cases, these regions readily adopted the *Equus caballus*, originally from central Asia.

At the time, the Sahara was filled with green oases. The region favored the evolution and growth of both men and horses. The Garamantian empire, mentioned in the writings of Herodotus, soon expanded to Libya, all the way to the big bend in the Niger River, near Gao. The political unity and economic prosperity that the empire enjoyed was linked to the great transportation system made possible by horses and carts. It was in northern Africa, above the great desert, that the first great cavaliers of the continent emerged. They were Numidian or Moorish, and rode with neither saddle nor bridle, using only a simple stick to lead their horses and a strap around their necks to stop them.

The African cavalry, which was born under the long reign of the Numidian King Masinissa (202–148 B.C.E.), eventually fought the armies of Carthage and later Roman troops. They had fierce guerrilla tactics: armed with javelins and daggers, protected by a light leather shield, the cavalrymen charged in jumbled formation, withdrawing and charging again until breaking enemy ranks. The Romans named them *Barbari*, or Barbarians—meaning foreigners—which became Berbers in English. And their horses became known as the Barbs.

During the second half of the eighth century, the heralds of Islam, who came from the East on their noble purebreds, built the holy city of Kairouan, in today's Tunisia, before setting out to con-

If this were not that the omnipotent being
feared by the planets
I would have traveled on the back of my horse
Through the dome of the universe.

ANTARA
Arab warrior and poet (fourth century),
hero of the epic titled *The Saga of Antar*

quer the Sunset Countries, the Maghreb. There, they discovered a hardy horse that was strong and perfectly adapted to nomadic life. Gradually, the horses were crossed and the Berbers adopted certain aspects of the equestrian practices of their invaders. Past masters in the art of the ambush, the latter joined the mercenary troops who would later erupt into the Old World.

The African horse emerged throughout the areas around the Mediterranean. Through crossbreeding, the Barb influenced the horse populations in these regions. Many writers and historians admired the horse's endurance, docility, and composure. The famous adage dates back to these times: "The Barb horse dies but never grows old." The horse was soon praised for its feats during the Crimean War. And in 1830, it was with the Barb that the Algerians resisted the attacks of the French cavalry.

Aware of the Barbs, the colonial troops systematized their breeding by creating the Remount Services and Equestrian Institutions of North Africa in 1852. The race became more and more established. To make them stronger, to give them more muscular bodies, they were crossbred with Syrian and Arabian purebreds. The first studbook on the Barb was recorded in Algeria as early as 1886, and then in Tunisia in 1896, and finally in Morocco in 1914. Omnipresent in northern Africa, the Barb, ready for all battles, all conquests, all struggles, has remained the loyal companion of the riders of fantasia, that art named "gunpowder game," or *baroud*, which stems from Numidian war strategies of the past. Today, peasants or nomads breed them less for plowing and transportation purposes than to sing the praises of the cavaliers and horses of the Maghreb.

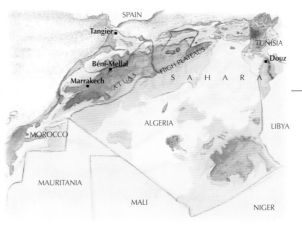

The costumes, harnesses, and rules of the fantasia vary from region to region. Even the riders of the Great Maghreb share the desire to perpetuate this equestrian art. They are all conscious of being its special guardians.

Passing through Tangier, Eugène Delacroix witnessed the encounter of two cavaliers. He wrote their story in a letter. "Immediately, the horses reared and confronted each other with such spite that I felt fear for the cavalrymen, although it was a splendid subject for a painting." In 1836, he immortalized the memory of this "fantastic and extraordinary" event. The painting would be known under the name *Fantasia Marocaine* (Moroccan Fantasy). In the foreground, there is a carabineer in a burnous, his horse rearing in the excitement of the battle. Behind, as if in a painted whirlwind, there is the image of an Arabian cavalry charging at top speed, as Delacroix had seen during the fantasias performed in honor of the mission of the Count of Mornay, with whom he went to Morocco.

More than 160 years later, the fierce splendor of the ancient Numidian warrior on whom the gold and silver jewels outline an arc of reverie, has not changed. The *fantasia* is surely one of the most moving spectacles one can see in the Maghreb.

During an afternoon in *moussem*, with the schistose slopes of the Atlas Mountains gleaming in the distance, the cavaliers converge on the plain, in little groups, their burnooses immaculate, their heads wrapped in turbans. The grass is orange, brown, maybe golden, but nowhere is it green. In some parts, the dust billows into thick, yellow clouds that lend an exotic Western air to the landscape. There are now

The horse is a house, his tufts are its foundations and the roof, his high head.

ARAB SAYING

more than a hundred of them waving their muskets, objects from an ancient gunsmith filled with black powder. In this surreal world, these princes from the *Arabian Nights* are now only shadows moving through a crowd that has come to cheer them on.

First, a silence that is heavy with anticipation and concentration. A husky cry. A command from the *mokhadem*, the leader. At his sides, ten riders line up in single file, shoulder to shoulder, standing on their wide stirrups. The horses swing their heads, rearing and pawing the ground with impatience. And then they charge, to the cry of *Al Hafid Allah*, "God the protector." It is a thunderous reminder of the fierceness of battles. With burnooses, turbans, and manes in the wind, the men and horses charge towards the imaginary enemy. They now abandon themselves to space in a furious gallop, in defiance of the stones and sand. At times, a solitary acrobatic feat is boldly and rashly performed.

The women ululate, drums beat, and shrill cries celebrate the rise of these wonderful cavaliers, their reins flowing, their muskets extended. Upon the order of the *mokhadem*, they simultaneously shoot. The bangs, like thunder, rise to the sky to the applause of an excited people. Then, with a merciless pull to the bit, the gallop comes to a sudden stop, only a few yards from the crowd. In the first rows, the audience, their bodies stiff, their faces grinning, seems to worry about their safety. But the cavaliers, being master horsemen, stop short. Another fantasia begins immediately in the dust, cries are let out, muskets are waved.

Until night falls, the bouts come one after the other, like incessant waves coming to die on a human cliff. Drunken

The Arabs have always preferred good horses to their own children, and they take so much delight in parading their horses during their holidays or gunpowder races, that they would rather deprive themselves of food than see them suffer from thirst or hunger.

BEN EL OUARDY
Arab poet

gallop, drunken gunpowder. The glorious memory of yesterday's warrior, for whom confrontation and combat were not yet symbolic.

The scene takes place near a village of Beni Mellal, at the foot of the Moroccan Atlas Mountains, during the Moulay Idriss *moussem*. But we could just as well be—with more or less splendor, and with slight variation—in the great plain of Marrakech, in the high Algerian plateaus, or in Douz, in the south of Tunisia. Throughout the Maghreb, and in Morocco in particular, fantasia riders gather for every *moussem*, for every religious or civil holiday. Their space is that which the Arab conquerors had named *Jaziret el Maghreb*, the "island of the setting sun." And this island, in the north of Africa, extends from the Atlantic to the shores of Cyrenaica, from the Mediterranean to the Sahara. That is, from Mauritania to Libya. Vast territory. There are many complex and different societies here, but all of them are built on a common ethnic foundation: the Berbers, who call themselves the *Imazighen*, or "free men."

A thousand years before our common era, their Numidian ancestors rode with neither saddle nor bridle, fighting against the invader in guerrilla wars that terrified even the Romans. When they began using stirrups, they wore them naturally very short, rising up on them to throw arrows and javelins. This riding technique was mastered by the Zenete tribe: wedged between the saddle's very high cantle and pommel, standing up on their sharp angles of their stirrups, these warriors, who were the most efficient of Islam, dominated in battle. They were the ones whom Arab leader Moussa ibn Nasser sent out, in 711, to conquer Spain, under the command of the Berber Rariq ibn Ziyad.

My horse leaps like a lion searching through the forest.
Or like a boat that, floating on the sea, takes off when
a wind fills its sails. He'll take flight with a squeeze
from my heel, he is the ornament leading the fantasias.

MESTFA BEN BRAHIM
Arab poet

This tent village, which is pitched
for a few days in the Moroccan
Atlas Mountains, houses the riders
of the Bemimquild tribe. They
will participate in the fantasias
scheduled during the ceremonies.

The "Zenetes mount," prevalent throughout the Maghreb, belongs to the *fantasia* riders.

The Arab historian Ibn Khaldun (1332–1406) undoubtedly paid the greatest homage to the Berbers, those seasoned warriors, experienced trainers and breeders: "They showed us such uncommon things, such admirable events, that it is impossible to not recognize the great care God has given them." For centuries, the practically undisturbed hideout of these scattered tribes was the long chain of the Atlas Mountains. Even today, it is in this high ground, behind the peaks and canyons, beyond the limestone ridges, in the shadows of the tangled narrow passes, that horses, passion, and man's knowledge retain the profound originality of the fantasia.

Asphalt has not yet been able to fight its revolution in the heart of these jebels, which are isolated by altitude. Neither has electricity—or hardly! There is only the muffled cry of the wind. The stab of the sun. Only the white of the sky hinging on the stone. And a dizzying view onto the valley below. In the midst of such harsh land, there rises a joy of life, a sense of beauty, even of the lavish, which has always inspired the Maghreb imagination. Carefully planned gardens pop up here and there; fennel and peppers grow in the shade of a palm tree. Each terrace is a wonder of color and fragrance.

Under the utterly gentle spring sun, the women weave wool rugs for their cube houses, the walls of which are crenellated like a fortress. Outside, on the steep path, little

girls play with hoops. Beside them, the family's donkey, shackled, feasts on a few blades of esparto grass. Later on, in the evening, it will bring the water from the wells. And Thursday, it will jog the women and children to the souk in the village. Rarely is the horse made to perform these tasks. If a horse were used, it would never be the one that is ridden on the day of *moussem*. For the stallion enjoys a special status: reserved for show, the horse is bred for the *fantasia*.

Here, the cavalier continues to take pride in the warrior qualities of his ancestors. He likes to talk about horses, gunpowder, the cries of the women . . . and he borrows a language from the heart, filled with honor and passion, from the great Arab poets:

My horse is the lord of horses.
A true drinker of air, he blackens our enemy's heart.
Remember that an ounce of honor
Is more than 100 kilos of gold.
Don't be fooled by anyone.
Leave the land in which your pride suffers
Leave it as soon as its walls are built with rubies.*

Symbol of pride, dignity, and independence, the horse of Barb and Arabian origin regains all its prestige during civil or religious celebrations in southern Tunisia.

*Text taken from the song of wandering poets published in the book *Chevaux du Sahara* (Horses of the Sahara).

Ask the night how many times I tore its veil,
Rode a horse with thinned sides and of stature.
Ask the desert, the hills, the valleys and the plains
The distance I have covered.
I wish only to fight the enemies
And to conquer their courageous cavaliers with mine.

EMIR ABD EL-KADER
Arab emir (1808–1883) who headed the resistance
against the Algerian conquest, from 1832 to 1847

Poetry is a good translator of this primal truth: a Berber, breeder of sheep, man of the Atlas Mountains, above all has the soul of a nomad. For him, the horse is not a distraction or, despite his love for splendor, a luxury object. The horse is an indispensable companion in his life of movement, struggle, and adventure, a life he loves, because the horse is independent, "Blessed by God and far from the sultans." Without this companion, a part of the world would crumble. How can you travel as a free man if not on a horse? How can you go with dignity to the souk if not on a noble horse? He goes on horseback even into the very heart of the rural regions of North Africa. For, to be a cavalier is to belong to a higher social class.

What patriarch Hadj Mohamed Sekri, the art dealer of fantasia, wants, and what he always gets, is "a fast and strong horse, a tough horse, a real warhorse": a Barb horse. He is aware that the latter is slower on the plain than an Arabian. But he doesn't care. The slope of the jebel, the

LEFT: *The lavish harnesses, costumes, and rifles, which are cared for with love, are passed down from generation to generation.*

BELOW: *While the rider gets ready, young Tunisian girls make sure the trimmings are just right.*

A good cavalier must know how much barley to give his horse, and how much powder to put in his rifle.

GENERAL E. DAUMAS
General Melchior-Jospeh-Eugène Daumas,
head of the Algeria Service for the Ministry of War.
Excerpt from *Chevaux au Sahara* (Horses of the Sahara), 1851

winter frosts and the summer droughts have given the horse resistance, endurance, and a confident step. This is the horse he loves. His place is in the courtyard of his master's house, where he lives under the attentive eye of the women. There, child and colt grow up together.

At two years old, the young stallion has already experienced a light bridle, a bit coated with honey, and boys enjoy hoisting themselves on its back. The following year, the horse is introduced to the saddle, then he is broken. He won't run in his first *fantasia* before the age of five or six. This is the amount of time that is necessary for training: the horse must grow used to crowds, and learn to tolerate sound, cries, and especially gunpowder. To arrive at this point, the master uses his instinct. Experience. Atavism.

"To be a reputable cavalier, it is not enough to know how to ride your horse. With rifle in hand, you need to be able to take advantage of a galloping horse on uneven terrain," the patriarch proclaims. He doesn't know the origins of the fantasia, which the Arabs call *laab* and *baroud*, the gunpowder game. His father, his grandfather taught him. His father also gave him the rifle and harness, made entirely of leather and wool, brocaded with gold thread and silk. As for the suit, it is carefully put away, with the war medal that the man earned for his feats against the French during the war of independence. The living memory of a people, a demonstration of bravery, the fantasia is above all satisfying to the man, who sums up his joy in this way: "Paradise is on a horse's back and in books. Or between a woman's breasts. The gunpowder is talking for them. What would they say if we didn't know how to fight? They wouldn't want to make couscous for us any more, preferring to serve more noble men than us."

The Cavaliers of Eternal Japan

JAPAN

The inheritors of a sacred ritual practiced by the Samurai, the archers
of the Empire of the Rising Sun, galloping on their horses to take up
a challenge that the common man would deem impossible.

History

Of all the animals of creation, the horse is the one to have the most durably filled man's imagination. For thousands of years, the nobility of its lineage and its mysterious character, which is both submissive and rebellious, have stirred up the most passionate emotions, the most extraordinary dreams, and the most amazing artistic creations. During the prehistoric period, when horses were mere game, the hunters were already depicting them on cave walls, using strong lines and often striking colors. The stone bas-reliefs of Nineveh, in Mesopotamia, record the feelings of pride and fear aroused by domestication, a major turning point in civilization.

For the first cavaliers who erupted from central Asia, into the West, the horse was not only a servant and companion of war and conquest: linked to the spiritual and the supernatural, the horse was part of the religious cult. Man and his horse were united until death. They made such a strong impression on foot-soldier populations and on pedestrians living along the Mediterranean coast that they gave rise to the fabulous centaurs. For a long time, in equestrian civilization, when a leader died, his horses were sacrificed. They would rest, marvelously harnessed, near his tomb, ready for the moment when he would awaken.

In India, the horse that is the victim—or the hero—of the sacrifice is the image of the cosmos itself: "The dawn is the head of the sacrificed horse. The Sun, his eye, the wind, his breath. The voracious fire is his open mouth. The celestial vault is his back, the sphere of space, his stomach . . . when he dies, he thunders. . . ." (sacred hymn of the Upanishads). The Vishnu temple, on an island in the Kaveri, is a monument that celebrates the equine species.

The symbol of perfect movement, the horse was also the greatest glory of the Greek world. At the beginning of mythology, it was the favorite animal of the gods and mortals. The chariot of the Sun's fire, the source of life, climbs up into the Mediterranean sky, led by four galloping horses. Pegasus, the winged horse, belongs to the in-

The knight says his horse is joyful in victory, mournful in defeat, participates in combat with all its might, and cries when his master has died.

JAQUES BOUDET

extricable maze of equestrian cosmology and the fantastic imagery of rituals. A true cavalier saga has unfolded, from the legendary Trojan horse to the no less legendary Bucephalus, the favorite horse of Alexander, who dedicated a city to him.

Rome, which attached great importance to its horses, built several equestrian statues. In Japan, painters gave their warhorses so much life that, at night, they left the screens they were decorating to graze on the garden grass. In China, where the horse was part of every aspect of life, the palaces of the emperors were filled with delicate figurines representing the Mandouch or Mongolian horses, brought to their stables. One of the most impressive treasures of this civilization is surely the terra-cotta army of soldiers, consisting of seven thousand life-sized mercenaries and six hundred horses, which populate the mausoleum of the first emperor Qin Shi Huangdi. Surely for reasons of economy,

the animal itself was quickly replaced by terra-cotta, bronze, and stone statues, or with bits, which were always placed under the head of the deceased.

The horse's moving beauty has been expressed everywhere, and man has not hesitated to use the horse to magnify himself. Their relationship goes beyond the level of reason and consciousness. Cavaliers sometimes form a class that has its corporate and elitist spirit, but none can escape the fundamental golden rule: the rule of established mutual trust. One of the equestrian arts that is truest to this image is without a doubt the *yabusame*, a martial art in the samurai tradition that dates back to the first millennium, and that continues today in the Japanese archipelago of pine forests filled with gods, wooden teahouses, and palaces, once built to celebrate the omnipotent masters, the shoguns.

*A martial art in the samurai
tradition, the yabusame is also a
magic ritual linked to Shintoism.
The Ogasawara and Takeda
schools alone perpetuate this
age-old equestrian art. More
than twenty yabusame events
take place every year in Japan,
always in sacred places.*

When the Japanese megalopolis buzzes and murmurs, when it becomes intoxicated with fever and noise, there are always a few retreats where eternal Japan retains its silences. A little garden edged with diaphanous bamboo, an oasis of calm disturbed only by the crow's cry, cherry tree blossoms under the cold winter sun. In two months, the tree will flower. The centaurs of the Rising Sun will gather under its branches, and all will prepare for the *yabusame* ceremony, the martial art in the samurai tradition, dating back to the first millennium. It is a perfect illustration of *Kyudo no michi*, literally the Way of the Bow and Horse, which preceded *Bushido*, the War of the Warriors. It is also a magical rite linked to Shintoism, which guarantees serenity for those who observe it.

There, just behind the miniature pond, a row of manicured shrubs indicates the path leading to the shrine that stands standing in its ideal garden. Inside their wooden and paper houses, the priests possess the tranquil assurance of knowledge. They know that their religion, founded on the cult of their ancestors and nature, is the oldest in the Japanese archipelago, and that their deities populate forests, waters, mountains, sky, and earth. First, there is the sun goddess, Amaterasu, who is at the origin of the land of the Rising Sun, so poetically named the Dragonfly Country, or the Country-of-the-river-of-autumn.

In present-day Japan, a triumphant Japan, a Japan of high technology, a Japan that was the third power in the world in

1968, only one century after the start of the Meiji era of "Enlightenment," modernism does not exclude tradition.

Beneath the interlacing highways that rise over the city, in the streets and avenues, people are massed together on the streets in tight rows. There isn't any pushing or shoving. But at every step they cross ghosts from age-old legends and, of course, countless *kamis*. These spirits are everywhere, housed in trees, lakes, torrents, caves, even in the minuscule rock that the Japanese visit in pilgrimages. They also use the smallest garden and the smallest intersection to live with humans and animals.

Beyond the labyrinth of cubes that are piled up between sea and long and massive mountains, topped by giant billboards or sky-high golf courses, this competitive and conquering world is made of white sand coves, pine forests and alleyways, of arched bridges, moss-covered lanterns and cafes. Thousands of cafes are flooded with images, but every night in November, the television broadcasts the maples turning red and, in March, the cherry trees blooming. What would beauty be, the Japanese say, if it were forever established? The cherry tree flower, the emblem of the samurai, symbolizes life's fragility. It is all the more beautiful that it is ephemeral: "Fallen from a branch, a

Before the ceremonies, the archers gather for a short prayer and are intensely engaged. The audience that has come to watch the event fully acknowledges the spiritual aspect of this perilous equestrian art.

*The warrior in his solitude gathers his arrows
and listens to the crackling icy plain.*

HAIKU
Short Japanese poem

flower returns to it: it's a butterfly," wrote Morikage, the haiku poet.

From the sacred ritual at the festival, from the tea ceremony to the bathing ceremony, from the arrangement of a flower bouquet to the arrow being released from the bow, it is a fascination, a profound joy, a learned alchemy of feeling that is at play. A contained feeling that becomes a great art, like archery. Master Anzawa (1887–1970) thought in these terms: "Archery has to take on a form that is wise and profound, great and supreme. The natural expression of the self through archery has to be the fulfillment of the unity of the three principles: the Truth, the Good, and the Beautiful. . . . If you wish to live in harmony with sky and earth, do not seek to reach the goal. Do not seek the pleasure of the goal, take the path of the union of body and soul."

In the ancient Chinese manuscripts, it is already specified that the Japanese used a long wooden bow with bamboo arrows. During the Nara period (710–794), mounted archery played an important role in the maintenance of and the search for a solemn attitude during the ceremonies that multiplied at the court. Then, noblemen tuned it in into a civic art, while the working class transformed it into a war discipline. In 1192, when Japan entered the Samurai era,

If you are asked about the Japanese soul, says the poet, you'll answer that it is the fragrance of the bloomed flower of the wild cherry tree at sunrise.

MOTOORI NORINAGA
Japanese poet

The master of ceremonies, the archers and target judges, the pennant and flag bearers, the arrow gatherers, and all the participants of the yabusame *don highly elegant costumes. They are subtle, embroidered with the family's coat of arms. Every stage of dressing stems from a sacred ritual.*

There is no greater loneliness than that of the samurai.

JAPANESE SAYING

The parade that precedes the first rounds are liturgical and take place on the runway. Its width is equal to the length of the arch, which is just over seven feet.

these warriors, under the influence of Zen, learned about detachment, which liberated them from combat as a solution. No longer worried about defeat or death, they were considered invulnerable.

The Imperial Restoration of 1868, which destroyed the power of the shoguns—the feudal lords who had maintained control of the kingdom for three centuries—sounded the death knell for the class of samurai. They subsequently lost all their privileges, but the samurai spirit lived on. It helped sustain the feeling of hierarchy that filled Japanese society and can still be found in the detailed ritual of protocols, presentations, and ceremonies. It is in this tradition that more than twenty *yabusame* events take place every year in Japan in sacred places. One event in particular unfolds on November 3 in Tokyo, where the greatest Japanese crowds gather in a celebration of the birthday of Emperor Meiji, the father of modern Japan. On this holiday, before

presiding over the ceremony, the master dons his ceremonial kimono and puts the *aya igassa* on his head, which goes with a warrior mask. While his horse grazes, he gets ready by meditating. In his world, breathing exercises are key to preparing the mind for the task ahead. He then enters the sacred place, on horseback, and points his bow and arrow first toward the sky, then toward the ground. He asks the gods for eternal peace for the elements and prosperity throughout the entire world. The competition can begin.

All at once, the target inspectors, the pennant and fan bearer, the arrow gatherers, and the drummer take their respective places along a roped runway. The cavaliers, magnificently armored in shells, bamboo, and wicker, canter in front of the targets to warm up their horses.

The fans are lowered to the beat of the drum, and the first cavalier goes to the end of the runway. There, as part of the ritual, he lets go of his reins on the horse's neck, and begins to gallop. His chest puffs up, he bends his bow, and begins to aim his arrow. This position requires deep abdominal breathing. The bow's cord gradually attains its maximum tension. A moment of pure beauty.

Only now does the archer stand up and turn his head toward the target. But he doesn't aim. The gesture is led by the intensity and concentration of the mind. All of a sudden, both arrow and cry are released in an amazing rush of adrenaline.

These slow and discreet movements, these sustained efforts are repeated three times in an attempt to hit the targets staggered across the runway with arrows. The cavalier's steel legs straddle the horse, which continues to run straight. After the third attempt, he sits back in his saddle and takes up his reins. At this point, his shoulders shadow the upward and downward movement of his mount. They undulate in the distance, as if they were a single being. Meanwhile, the second archer appears at the beginning of the runway.

The rules of the *yabusame* have not changed in more than a thousand years. The stunning costumes and enameled harnesses, inlaid with mother-of-pearl and gold, have retained all of their splendor. This taste for luxury, this extreme refinement, this ostensible opulence are not innocent: they were in past times the prerogative of the lords who formed a tiny fraction of the class of samurai—

Our lord is a god, and the paddy fields where the roan horses crawled, is where he made his capital.

POEM BY OTOMO NO MIYUKI
Japanese poet

At the crossroads between body and spirit, the yabusame *requires a great deal of concentration and ardor. The goal of this art is not only to master perfect marksmanship, the "Self," but to find one of the many ways to "light."*

A warrior's child awakens to the sound of the bridle.

JAPANESE PROVERB

all the others lived modestly, even in poverty, for they were only remunerated according to their feats as warriors. The *yabusame* ritual, which they performed after having sworn absolute loyalty to their overlord, took place inside a sacred temple. The three targets represented war, power, and peace. And the results of the hits were interpreted as omens indicating the favor of the gods. Subjected to an implacable honor code, a samurai who missed a target would immediately surrender himself to death.

In our day, only the ceremonial shots and the spiritual values attached to *yabusame* have been preserved. The archers try to outdo anyone they meet, accepting a challenge that the layman would consider impossible: to hit all the targets, which are less than four inches in diameter by the final round. The archers are further judged on all-around movement, style, and rapidity of execution. The winner is asked to kneel before the master of ceremonies and carry the target pierced by his last arrow in his hands. In return for his merit, the master looks at him through his fan.

Located at the crossroads of body and spirit, where their forces are in harmony, the *yabusame* requires years of training under the kind guidance of a great master. The apprenticeship is intense, restrictive, rigorous. But it is what the student needs if he wants to progress down the Way of the Bow and Horse, so that one day, he can perhaps attain Supreme Beauty. It's a form of asceticism, a theology of gesture. History only makes a very brief mention of the big names in the discipline, including members of the Ogasawara and Takeda families, who founded the two schools of *yabusame* that continue the tradition today. The sublime is attained when the master, reaching the final stage of his art, lays down the bow and arrow, never to use them again.

The magnificent costumes and harnesses, made entirely of bamboo, lacquered wood, and embroidered silk, were once the prerogative of lords who formed a tiny fraction of the class of samurai.

The Dancers of Andalusia

SPAIN

A Spanish rhapsody of sound, costume, and fragrance, the proud city of Jerez de la Frontera shows all of its colors. It is dedicated to Spanish purebreds, with its Royal School, its ferias, its *vaqueros*, and its *ganaderias*.

On the Iberian peninsula, the figures painted in the prehistoric caves point to a close bond between the first hunters and wild horses. You can recognize the powerful neck, the short limbs and mane of the animals that represent the Mongolian wild horse. Domesticated, then mounted during the second millennium, the horse later emerged throughout the areas around the Mediterranean. In Numidia and in Libya, the beauty of its forms were repeatedly praised. But it was its vocation for battle that would make the horse the protagonist of the West's military history.

There are numerous citations in literature and in the history of antiquity that stress the skill with which the cavaliers exploited the manageability of their horses. They followed the example of Xenophon, who, in *Hellenica*, describes the revolutionary techniques of the mercenaries fighting for Sparta at the end of the Peloponnesian War: "They charge at full speed against the enemy and bring their horses to a sudden stop when face to face with them. Then, they make an about-turn to take some distance and charge again and fight with swords."

Humiliated by the skill of the Arab and Berber squadrons who, in the year 711, crossed the Strait of Gibraltar, the Spanish Christians placed all the more importance on the mobility and speed of intervention. Their saddles were high, their stirrups were short and sharp, their bits severe, their spears light. And their riding technique, known as *jineta*, was borrowed from the Berber cavaliers of the Zenete people. It was a technique that noblemen would ceaselessly refine throughout the *Reconquista*. At the same time that Andalusian horses—the pure Iberian breed, a descendant of the Barb—were being bred, bulls were being reared. Therefore, the interest that Spaniards have in bullfighting clearly dates back to the earliest years of Antiquity. For this is the true definition of *jineta* riding: a battle against man, but also a battle against animal. At that time already, armor was being replaced by embroidered velvet, by toques and capes.

Because the Iberian horse is energetic, the Neapolitans of the

*Today your blood gallops throughout the world because your line is so old
that it shines as more genuine than the sun. You are the horse of History;
Velazquez, in the canvas of his glory, painted "your pure Spanish race."*

ANGEL PERALTA
Spanish writer and poet, bull breeder and rejoneador (born in 1926).
Excerpt from the poem, "My Companion"

fifteenth century, under the authority of Ferdinand, King of Aragon, were easily able to defeat the heavy French palfreys. By the sixteenth century, the horsemen of the kingdom of Naples had laid down the foundation of a methodical style of riding. The art of *manège* was born. Andalusian horses became the mount of choice for kings and emperors. They were the height of fashion throughout the princely and royal courts of Europe. An ideal model for classical equitation, Andalusians were the prestigious ancestor to Lusitanos, Lipizzaners, and other breeds. They were also the horses who crossed the Atlantic with the conquistadors and were at the root of the amazing repopulation of horses in the New World. The Andalusian horse was therefore in a state of grace. The harmony of its forms and its aspect inspired the greatest of artists, including Velázquez, Van Dyck, and Rubens. Until the end of the eighteenth century, no other breed would be more often depicted in engraving and

painting. But in a Spain that was in the grip of civil wars, fashion and necessity forced European breeders to turn to Nordic and Neapolitan stallions. Their goal was to produce hardier horses, especially for farming. The blossoming taste for races and jumping, which came from across the Channel, contributed to the decadence of academic riding and, as a result, to the decline of the Andalusian horse. Eventually the Spanish horse was used only for refined dressage teams and the prestige of the *paseos*.

In 1864, when management of Spanish breeding was transferred to the Ministry of War, the stallion herds were placed under the good care of the army. Hope had been restored. And yet it was not until 1978 that the Iberian horse was acknowledged as a separate breed. It has only been after much effort that contemporary Andalusian breeders have been able to bring what were once the most beautiful horses of Christianity to the fore of the equestrian scene.

Between the vineyards and the olive fields, Spanish purebreds and toros bravos *share the space and light of the vast lands of the Guadalquivir plain. Riders are at the very heart of Andalusian life.*

With its sweet and tortuous name like an arabesque on its side, *Andalucía* rings of a separate world. A land of shadows and light, of passions. The land of Federico García Lorca and Manuel de Falla. From the banks of the Guadalquivir to the banks of the Guadalete, there is a single bedazzlement, rigorous and severe, a regular rhythm that beats from the green of olive trees, the black of soil, the white of houses. Dotting the landscape, in the blaze of its whitewashed walls, a hacienda sparkles in the sun.

It's here that we find Jerez de la Frontera, the proud, the beautiful Andalusian woman. Jerez as nobility. This is the land of lords, inheritors of the *latifundia*, which were, in their time, the fortune of the Romans. There is nothing so obvious, so primordial as these hills and valleys where vineyards and olive trees cover the black ground with soft shadows. And there is always impeccable alignment, symmetrical rows that divide the neat expanses of the pastures.

The former province of Baetica, and its natural resources were all that was needed to feed, along with Tunisia, the entire Roman population. It enjoys a privileged climate and the fertility of its soil has been celebrated for thousands of years. No one can deny that it is the home of an age-old equestrian tradition. How did this land, a melting pot of many civilizations, watch the birth of these horses, which were the height of fashion in all the princely and royal courts of Europe? The horizons are boundless.

*Nestled against the banks of the
Guadalete, the Cartuja monastery
in Jerez is the birthplace of the
most prestigious of the Spanish
purebred line: the cartujano. The
Carthusian monks live here, but
their horse breeds have been
widely separated.*

Indeed, as early as the sixteenth century, the monks of
the Cartuja Carthusian monastery in Jerez provided patient
care and applied their skill to breeding the horses that were
for a long time considered to be the best in the world.
Favoring the purity of the Andalusian race, they rejected everything from Barb, Arabian, or Neapolitan breeds. Their
horses were branded with a bell, which, in the eighteenth
century, was replaced with the image of a bit. After the religious orders disbanded in Spain, the monks were forced to
leave the Jerez monastery and to sell their horses. There were
many complicated transactions between the Jerez breeders.
But the cartujano line would remain the most admired among
the different descendants of the purebred Spanish horses.

It is for this reason that, today, when the day breaks over the banks of the Guadelete, emotions are intense. On one side, there is the Jerez monastery, still, silent, secret. On the other, more than 250 graceful silhouettes, silver manes, and snow-white coats, dot the pastures: mares and colts bear the mark of Cartuja breeding. The stables and rings are nearby, on the land of La Fuente del Suero. Since 1990, this horse farm run by the State has been responsible for the upkeep of the cartujano horse, the genetic heritage considered indispensable to improving the Spanish purebred. This endeavor comes after a genuine renaissance of Iberian horses, which were kept by elite riders like the Portuguese master Nuno Oliveira and his students, who were prominent figures in the breeding and bullfighting world. Indeed, in Spain and elsewhere, the Anglomania of the nineteenth century, and then the trend of horseback riding as a sport, contributed to the decline of academic riding and, as a result, the decline of the Andalusian horse. The horse became folkloric and only great families of tradition kept them as a precious asset. These families included the Domecq dynasty, which owned up to 38,000 acres of land between the Guadalquivir and the Guadelete.

For this reason, in 1972, Don Alvaro Domecq, the first *rejoneador* of Spain, who regretted that his province, the bastion of the art of horses, could no longer keep its traditions alive, founded the Royal Andalusian School of Equestrian Art, which is known worldwide today. It stands in the heart of Jerez, within the palace of Recreo de las Cadenas.

Here there also stands the castle that the Duke of Abrantès built last century using Garnier, the French architect, who had also built the Opéra in Paris. The new stables were star-shaped with a round tack room in the center. The adjoining ring is remarkably elegant, with walls decorated with *azulejos*. There is seating room for up to sixteen hundred spectators, and, as is proper, there is a special loge reserved for the king of Spain. Every week, it is in this tradition-filled environment that the famous equestrian ballet world is performed: *Como Bailan Los Caballos Andaluces* (How Andalusian Horses Dance).

This school, designed as a true academy of traditional equestrian art, seeks to train riders of high standing, like those from the Spanish Riding School of Vienna. Many of these riders have already stood out in international compe-

By front view or profile, calm, fleeting,
White, pure and large, innocent.
Divine and growing rays of light,
Blind and profound harmony at a gallop,
You are the great immortal horses,
Children of the son and musical lather.

RAFAEL ALBERTI
Spanish poet and painter (1902–1999)

You, Spanish horse, great "cartujano"
You adorn yourself in fiery gaits
Your mane is the wind's caress
And your back is a sovereign throne.

ANGEL PERALTA
Spanish writer and poet, bull breeder and rejoneador (born in 1926).
Excerpt from the poem, "My Companion"

titions of classical dressage, such as Rafael Soto, artistic director, who placed seventh at the Olympic Games in Atlanta; or Ignacio Rambla, three-time champion of Spain in dressage, who ranked tenth at the Atlanta Olympics in the grand prix and eleventh in Kür with his horse Evento (born in 1985 in the Yeguada Militar of Jerez). Once you become aware of the difficulties of this classical discipline, as well as the ostracism of Spanish purebreds in modern competitive dressage, these results seem all the more remarkable.

But the Royal School does more than prepare for shows and competitions. By teaching classical equitation and *doma vaquera* (riding *vaquero* style), the school is passing down the most complete of Andalusian traditions to the next generation of masters. Some have opened their own equestrian centers, visited by riders from all different backgrounds. Others work with of promising horses that belong to the best breeders in the region. There is strong motivation to have the purebred Spanish horse at the top of the equestrian scene again.

When it comes time for the ferias, the city of horses buzzes with traditions that are the pride of Jerez. Throughout the peninsula, horses and *jinetes* (cavaliers) don ceremonial clothing. It is a Spanish rhapsody of sound, costume, and fragrance. The Andalusian heart never stops beating.

The feria? It used to be the livestock fair, a huge rural market for cattle and horses, who were made shiny and elegant in order to seduce buyers. The horses also had to have great bearing, *gracia*, the training to perform kinds of movements, and to be perfectly mannered. The present-day

> *A prince is never surrounded by as much majesty*
> *on his throne as he is on a beautiful horse.*

WILLIAM CAVENDISH,
Duke of Newcastle

In the center of the city of Jerez,
the former palace of the Duke
d'Abrantès, known as the "Recreo
de las Cadenas," is now home to
the Royal School. The muffled
sound of riders, the steady breath
of horses … During the morning
training, they prepare magnificent
ballets.

festival goes by the same name, but today, it is a living example of a culture and customs that Jerez will never relinquish.

Every year, the first feria comes with the spring. As early as the month of March, the haciendas, the hamlets, the villages, every family helps prepare for the festivities. Priority is given to the horses, which the breeders and the *jinetes* train so that they are in top shape for the competitions, each in its own discipline: *doma vaquera*, jumping, and *acoso y derribo* (equestrian technique meant to measure the bravery of bulls), dressage, vaulting, carriage driving, endurance, and, of course, the bullfights, from which come national celebrities.

The riders of the Royal School devote themselves to the final rehearsals of the splendid gala that takes place at the Recreo de las Cadenas. Because of its pure equestrian quality, and also because of the quality of horses that participate, Jerez's is certainly the most important feria in Spain.

The municipality sets up a *real* in the middle of the city,

The Royal School of Jerez is known as an academy of traditional equestrian art. During shows, riders don the Andalusian costume from the eighteenth century. The saddles and bridals, however, are royal in style.

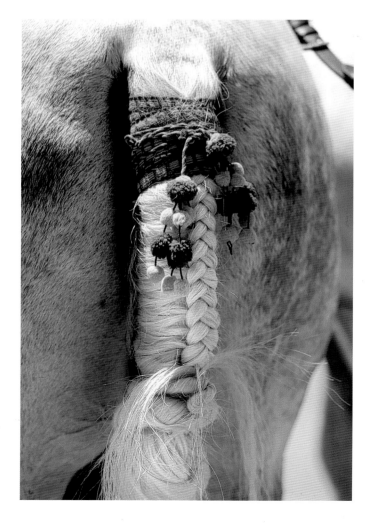

The purebred is branded on its thigh with the emblem of the farm from which it came. It has abundant, fine, and shiny hair that is braided when the horse is hitched to a carriage.

The equestrian ballet of the Royal School of Jerez displays all the expressions of dressage and the classical school of equitation, as well as the figures that belong to traditional Andalusian equitation, in particular the doma vaquera.

I class the true Spanish horse as the greatest, offering him my voice as to the most handsome, the most noble, the bravest and most worthy of kings.

SALOMON DE LA BROUE (1530–1610),
Riding master for Henri IV
Citation from *Le Cavalerice Français,*
2nd Edition, Paris, 1602.

in the Gonzalès Hontoria park. It consists of more than two hundred *casetas*, or little houses, lined up along the wide paths. For a long time, they have been reserved for breeders, local clubs and institutions, posh associations and large wine families. They decorate and arrange these *casetas* as they would their own houses, with furniture, rugs, knick-knacks, stereos, a kitchen, and provisions. For eight days, all they do is eat, talk, dance, and drink. *Fino, manzanilla, amontillado, oloroso*, the sherry of Jerez, amber like a sunny day, are a part of every moment of Andalusian life. It's a miniature city built overnight, a city that is at all times reserved for pedestrians and cavaliers. Display is part of the ritual, and nothing is too beautiful for it.

First come the sparkling brass carriages led by four, six, and sometimes eight plumed horses. Then there is the procession of *caballeros*, driving their horses at a Spanish walk or before the school of classic equitation to exhibit their talent. The women, wearing flounce dresses and mantillas, are invited to ride on the backs of the horses. Here more than anywhere, the Andalusian women justify their reputation: dancing from *caseta* to *caseta*, they are at every moment carried by the sound of guitars and vocal arabesques. They clap their hands, play castanets, and dance. And all the languor, the din of flamenco, speaks to their deepest memories, to their ancestors, who continue to live in them. Andalusians love the country in which they were born. They are so proud that they praise it, venerate it for all of its vigor.

Nevertheless, cavalier life is more than parade and celebration. The daily aspect is what gives it meaning. You have to seek this primal truth in the *ganaderias*, in which bullfighting equitation and *doma vaquera* were founded.

During the feria, men, women, and children try to outdo each other in joyful elegance. Displaying oneself is part of the ritual and there is nothing that is too beautiful for the occasion. Whether on foot, horse, or carriage, everyone strolls up and down the paseo, *which is lit day and night by garlands of light.*

Next to the vineyards, horses and bulls share the space and light of the vast estates of the Guadalete plain. They are branded on their thigh, the mark of their "home," their coat of arms. They belong to the great families of Jerez, the remaining members of the local aristocracy, and they bear the name Domecq, Peralta, Garcia, Delgado, or Mendez. Their vocation is breeding the *toro bravo*, the large arena bull. Knowledge and passion are passed down from father to son, a kind of heritage that has spanned the generations and will survive.

The Last *Cimarrones*

COLOMBIA—VENEZUELA

Breeders, nomads, and cavaliers, they are committed to the age-old

occupation of their desert land. Their semiwild horses simultaneously

represent wealth and social status and are the trading currency.

They are the silent Indians of the *Guajira*.

Christopher Columbus's seventeen caravels, which set sail from Cádiz on September 25, 1493, had twenty-four Andalusian stallions and ten mares on board, part of a huge freight of agricultural and military goods. This is how the horse was brought back to the continent of its origins, America, the birthplace it left at the dawn of humanity. The first American breeding farm was founded seven years later on the Island of Hispaniola, present-day Haiti. Others followed in Cuba, Puerto Rico, and Jamaica. The Andalusian horse was the instrument of conquest for the Spaniards who arrived in large numbers.

It does not seem that the Amerindians of the Caribbean were particularly impressed by this strange animal. They had seen so many things ever since the large ships came to their shores, bringing war, destruction, and slavery, that nothing surprised them anymore. Shining armor, weapons that make lightning, pale and hairy faces. . . . Therefore, the quadrupeds upon which the invaders rode seemed no stranger than the steers, sheep, and goats they had not known until that point.

Yet, when Cortez invaded Mexico in the spring of 1519, the Aztecs were genuinely terrified by the fifteen cavaliers that accompanied him. In their eyes, man and animal were one, a kind of centaur. The same was true with the Incas when Pizarro's soldiers went into action. "Fear grew when a cavalier fell from his horse. The Incas thought that the being had divided in two, and such a miracle made them lose their minds," reports W. H. Prescott, in *The History of the Conquest of Mexico*.

The mystery and strength emanating from the horse were the conquistadors' secret weapon. But the animal fled, finding freedom in the immense plains, reproducing as if in a paradise it had lost. The Indians soon learned the benefits that they could reap from the horses. Following the example of the Chacos Indians of Mexico, some began hunting them for leather and meat. Others attempted

A warrior's best friend is a good horse, and what a warrior wishes most is that his horse be as swift as a swallow when dodging an enemy, or when charging ahead.

LONE MAN

to ride them. As early as 1600, the Plains Indians used horses for transportation, for pulling the travois, which until that point was reserved for dogs. Not having the Spanish model, the Indians had to reinvent everything, in order to tame and train the animals they named Sho-a-thinga, Mistatim, Sunke Wakan, It-Shouma-Shunga—Amazing Dog, Big Dog, Dog of Mystery, Red Dog. . . .

From Tierra del Fuego to the Canadian prairies, the horse became part of Indian religion, war, and home. In time, it differed from its Andalusian ancestors in its morphology and color, becoming stronger and more muscular. It is said that at this time the Nez Percé tribe, of the fertile Northwest region created the Appaloosa—the name comes from the Palouse River—with its traditional speckled coats. Its docility, beauty, and originality were fought over for a long time. The explorers Lewis and Clark encountered Appaloosas for the first time at the begin-

ning of the nineteenth century and said that "these horses were equal if not superior to all that could be found in the pastures of Virginia." But there were few Indian ethnic groups that took interest in breeding. Capturing and taming mustangs enhanced the prestige of the warrior. Stealing horses from the enemy was undoubtedly the most noble way to obtain the animal. Some Indians rode bareback, guiding their horses with a leather cord wrapped around the lower jaw. Others, such as the Sioux and the Comanches, used saddles and bridles.

Finding the perfect balance for every use of the horse, the Indians of America established a matchless reputation as horsemen. Some Europeans nicknamed them "red devils"; others talked about "the best light cavalry in the world." The horse became the splendor of these martyred people, who lived through ages without abdicating any of their pride.

Discrete, rustic, and sturdy, the horses of the Wayuu Indians live almost in the wild in herds. Only the best are chosen for equestrian events. Hence their name cimaroones, *which, in colonial America, designated fugitive slaves.*

Nothing moves. It's a far away country, a land of silence and distance moving towards the Caribbean Sea, like a flat and stripped racket. A peninsula burned by the sun, filled with candelabra cactus and scrawny acacias bent by the trade winds. The image of the *Guajira*, the land of the Wayuus Indians, is striking. Everywhere are prickly bushes that dry out without dying, or that die after having entrusted their seeds with the survival of the species until the next rain. Everything is pale. Everything blurs together. The wild billows and the marshes, the humid beaches and hard ground, the sand and rock.

The beauty is austere. There, nearby, a dried-up stream escapes toward the horizon and disappears, like sight. Then, in the distance, silhouettes rippling in the waves of heat catch your eye. A convoy of donkeys. They are crossing the plain, single file. Some are carrying a mountain of cans; others are ridden by women draped in long veils. They all amble along. Undoubtedly, it's a matter of scale: in a landscape of this size, even a galloping horse would look lazy.

Everyday at the same hour, the women go to the wells and a group of goats returns. Others arrive, at least fifty of them, red, white, speckled, tall, pushing and shoving, heading straight for their destination. A veil of dust masks the ground trodden by the animals. Behind the prickly bush where they wait impatiently, three beams form a triangle

Lightning has wings and leads a horse.

INDIAN PROVERB

over a deep, wide hole dug in the subterranean waterbed. The first rains of September will turn it into a torrent.

A teenager, his strong body visible beneath an open shirt, pulls up the pail that he pours into a hollowed tree trunk. His movement is measured, regular, as if he had been repeating them since time immemorial. The pails come one after the other, the water spurts, the watering place fills and empties. Six donkeys, two mules, and three cows with hollow sides drink. Taking their distance, camouflaged in a cactus forest, there are disheveled horses and a colt glued to its mother. They are waiting their turn, with ferocious eyes and taut muscles. Flight is imminent. These are the *cimarrones* – brown slaves, fugitives. This was the term used in the past by Spanish colonizers to designate everything they subjugated, man and beast. It is a term that the Wayuus Indians still use to designate their horses. Half wild, yes. But they have an unparalleled reputation. This is how the Argentinian historian Angel Cabrera described them in 1947: "The peninsula of the *Guajira* contains the most authentic descendants of horses from the conquest, characterized by a running walk or a lateral four-beat gait, by exceptional ruggedness and courage . . ."

Close by, in the shade of a *trupillo* (type of acacia tree), are several dogs and shepherds. Almost motionless, they wait. They wait and they watch. The order in which the horses cross the finish line determines the order in the next race. Leaning against the rough trunks, suspended between dreaming and awakening, the shepherds keep track of their animals out of the corner of their eyes. The oldest isn't even sixteen years old. Some are obviously together; others seem to be ignoring each other as if there were some tension. Most of them carry a rifle over their shoulder sheathed in a leather holster, which protects it from the sand. They don't have revolvers; they are too young. And, in any case, the guns would be hidden inside their shirts. The men can defend themselves: a basic requirement for the existence of the clan.

The Wayuus and the *Guajira* are part of the same mystery. Both have a furtive presence and are hidden from others. The worried faces of the women, their faces painted up to their eyes in red or black to protect them from the sun. The hard, fixed looks from the men. The Indians are silent and isolated in their world. They are determined to care for the land, as they have been doing for hundreds of years. Their horizon is dotted with headstones, white, cube-shaped, imperious. Their houses, made of cactus wood and earth, are planted like so many fortresses in the middle of the desert, a maze of bare paths with intermittent patches of dry grass. The presence of living things seems obtrusive. However, nearly eighty thousand Wayuus live here, on this shared peninsula between Colombia and Venezuela. They have

Every day at the same hour, the cimarrones *head toward the watering place. After rain, a few temporary lakes are available to them. But quite often, they quench their thirst at the wells, when the shepherd comes to give water to his goats.*

never acknowledged the border between the two countries. The *Guajira* is their territory, and the Conquest didn't alter their existence, except for introducing breeding.

"These Indians became experts in stealing horses and other livestock, being fierce cavaliers, perhaps invincible . . ." wrote the historians of the Conquest. All of the attempts made by royal officers, missionaries, or explorers to interfere were doomed to fail. And still today, outsiders, the "non-Wayuus," the *alijunas*, rarely dare to venture into their territory. Traditions here are harsher than the drought, and the water more precious than gold.

These Indians of Arawak origin who became breeders, nomads, and riders, stayed faithful to their rituals, their culture, and their beliefs. First there were the supernatural beings, a source of almost daily preoccupation and torment. Then Ka'i, the Sun, the master of horses, became the only distinctive symbol of power and prestige. Then came the godsend—goats, sheep, cows, and donkeys—that Maleiwa, the Creator, had long ago divided up between the thirty-five matrilineal clans that make up their society.

Livestock plays an essential role in the tangible world of the Wayuus, in their daily life when they hunt, fight, celebrate, and grieve. Meat and milk form the basis of their food resources. But by selling livestock they knew how to make an economic link with the outside world and to become integrated into the free market. Those who preferred to be self-employed in the salt mines in Manaure or to accept a job in the coal mines in Cerrejon or Maracaibo, one of the urban monsters in Venezuela, usually have only one idea in mind: to support the means to develop breeding or at the very least, to maintain it.

Whether it is a matter of survival, marriage, burial, or conflict between individuals or between clans, goats, cows, and donkeys always play a significant role. As do the horses, of course. They are both wealth and currency, and the number a man owns indicates his social standing. The Wayuu who attends a festival on horseback will immediately be recognized as a person of importance, almost a cacique, or chief. Purebred *cimarrones* will be saddled, but they are ridden only when food is abundant. They are lassoed when thirst drives them to a watering hole on days when the owner is authorized to use the wells. Their mythological origin might explain their name, *ama* in the Arawak language, since they are the sons of the *irama*, native to the

A symbol of wealth, prestige, and power, the stallion is well attended to. But he is only ridden in periods of abundance, when the rains renew life in the dry steppes.

God sleeps within stones, breathes among plants, dreams with animals, and awakens in humanity.

INDIAN PROVERB

The very elaborate harness is among the most precious of the Wayuu belongings. A man who attends a wedding or funeral on a horse is seen as an important figure, even a cacique (chief).

peninsula. The steed is also the totemic animal of the Epinayus, "those who strike the ground with force when they walk." No enclosure defines the clan's territories, which spread over the entire peninsula. A horse's skull, or that of another domestic animal, is suspended from a tree and is more than enough to keep away evil spirits.

It seems like another planet; the sand, the rock, and the dust gave way to a brush- covered steppe, where grass has taken root. In the distance are several mountains that resemble a pile of ashes. More quickly than the glimmer of dawn, a barely audible melody rises in the air. Birds are rustling and twittering. There are hundreds of them in this desert, and they all know how to survive where they can.

Then an imperious, prehistoric squawking gradually becomes louder. Under the roofs of branches balanced on four posts, a short distance from the delicate house made of a mixture of clay and straw where hammocks hang at night, a group celebrates a son's return. The flowerlike elegance of the women under their black and white veils, the great presence of the men with bronzed torsos, loincloths belted by woven wool with tassels.

Smiling faces painted in monochromatic, geometric designs: red, ochre, blue. From hand to hand they pass glasses of *chirinchi*, the local alcohol made from sugarcane. All around them waves of humid heat transform the plain into a transparent sea upon which the cavaliers seem to float. The harnesses are very elaborate, made of leather and wool, copper and horsehair—clearly the most precious thing that the Wayuus possess.

As one, the audience moves toward a grove of *trupillos*, the starting line for the race. The season is favorable for these festivities reserved for ceremonies, marriages, and burials—festivities that last more than a month sometimes, intended to counter the potential feelings of revenge of the deceased.

On the way, two distinct groups form, escorted by the riders. Each one is led by a narrator speaking at first in a sorrowful tone: "The drought is the worst enemy of the Wayuus. It brings hunger and death, but our horses are strong." This is followed by detailed praise of the steeds, their owners, and their riders. As from time immemorial the race is fought two by two, and the battles come one after the other. The colorful horse is held in high esteem, because "he is equal to the race as much as the steed whose color his coat resembles."

Without further ado, the deep and deafening drumbeats

When it comes time to leave,
I will come back to see you.
A great cloud will descend from the skies
And will envelop us, and thus our
Destination will remain secret.

APACHE POEM

announce the *yonna* dance. The couple that is performing mesmerizes the audience. The chassé steps of the young, veiled girl accelerate to the point where she almost loses her balance. And her partner ends by falling on the ground to enthusiastic yelling. The men raise their glasses. The male dancer is immediately replaced . . . no truce in the battle of the sexes.

Dances and secrets, a drum and storytellers, more than enough goat meat and boiled corn. Even soaked with corn beer and *chirinchi*, men and women maintain their dignity, more surprising than ever. And as expected, before the end of the day, as soon as ochre turns to gray, each person will withdraw under a roof and take care to close the windows and doors. The entire peninsula goes into a kind of torpor, which it won't emerge from until daybreak.

It's the right time of day to search through collective memory. It's the time to listen to the stories of the elders,

At the heart of this matrilineal society, the women hold the power within the household. Their main activity is weaving hammocks on vertical looms. The men tend to and supervise the livestock.

We are the invisible ones, the People of the Sky, the dream people whose voices are never touched by sorrow.

DEBRA CALLING THUNDER

During the day, the Wayuus hang their hammocks in the shade, beneath an awning of branches where family activities take place. At dusk, they bring them into their cob houses, which make them feel peaceful and safe.

The four winds blow, and the horses come in great numbers.

INDIAN PROVERB

who recline in hammocks as they share the heritage passed down from their forefathers. It's an opportunity for the Wayuus to confirm their beliefs in the spirits of the dead.

Outside there is no one, no light, no sound, only the haunting song of invisible insects. The desert is now "the kingdom of ghosts and messengers of death." It is said that these are the ancestors who roam. The soul actually leaves the body when the deceased can travel to Cabo de la Vela where Jepíra is located, "the land of dead Indians." Dressed in dark cloaks, walking a little as if they are drunk, they are vindictive, short-tempered, and they shoot arrows, which bring sickness, unhappiness, and death. In these extreme situations the Wayuus turn to the shaman, the specialist in communicating with spirits.

The night is dark; showers of stars fall through the sky. A distance away, the meager glow from a campsite seems like the only living thing in this world. It is time to dive into the world of dreams, the only place where the souls of dead Indians can meet those of the living to share knowledge. That's the way it is in the everlasting America of the Wayuu Indians.

The Princes of Vienna

AUSTRIA—SLOVENIA

The Spanish Riding School of Vienna still practices the classic art of riding in all of its purity. For four hundred years, generations of horsemen have continuously celebrated the myth of the centaur. Their white stallions, originally from Slovenia, are admired worldwide.

Medieval Europe made the horse into an instrument of war. But the nobility of the animal didn't become affected, because it was in battles associated with knights, which saved it from work in the fields. During a tournament it was protected with heavy armor, lavishly decorated, but little importance was given to the perfection of its form. Its stout build was strong and massive, and its training was perfunctory.

At the end of the fifteenth century, King Ferdinand V of Spain set out to recapture the kingdom of Naples. During the century that followed, the legendary skill of the Spanish cavaliers prevailed over the cumbersome armor of the French knights of King Charles VIII. At that time, Italy made its mark by making a change in its approach to riding horses, inspired by the delicacy and obedience of the Andalusian horse. Thus was born the art of classical equitation.

The first riding academy was established in 1532 by the Neapolitan aristocrat Federico Grisone. The carousel tunes come form the exercises the knights had to perform in order to prepare for battle: walk, trot, gallop, piaffe, pirouette, passage, and so on. After carefully studying the works of the Greek general Xenophon, Grisone soon wrote his manual, *Gli Ordini di Cavalcare* (The Rules of Riding). It was published in six languages and horrified people everywhere because it contained some brutal riding techniques. The fame of his school broke barriers, and several years later, Naples was considered to be the best school for expert riding.

Afterwards other academies sprang up in Naples, Rome, and Ferrara, including those of César Piachi and his student Jean-Baptiste Pignatelli who would train a host of famous riders and instructors. Kings and princes from the courts in Paris, London, Madrid, Dresden, Hanover, and Vienna flocked to see these masters and discover the secrets of the classical equitation. With the emergence of this new style, which was simultaneously artistic, scientific, and literary, the former tournament games lost

If a horse becomes restive because he has been overfed and constrained, it will become necessary to use as much gentleness and ceremony as when he was a colt. The rider will have talk to the animal's resources, his memory, and to his ability to see and hear.

LA BROUE

From *Le Cavalerice Français*, 2nd Edition, Paris, 1602.

their most ardent supporters. The academy combined all of the qualities necessary to this new art and its grace and delicacy satisfied the taste for luxury in that era. "It's the most beautiful horse in the world and the most suitable for a king on his day of triumph," wrote the duke of Newcastle of England, who gave the world of horsemen his *New Method and Extraordinary Inventions for Training Horses*, published in 1658.

The art of riding aimed for beauty and harmony down to the smallest detail. Through patient training, the rider searches for perfection in performing the spectacular movements such as levades, pesades, and caprioles. Equestrian academies flourished all over Europe and each teacher developed his own methods of teaching the horses and riders. There were great innovators, such as Löhneyssen, the first in a long line of German equestrian writers, Salomon de La Broue, the French author of the first treatise on the art of equitation, and

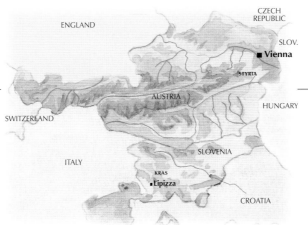

Antoine de Pluvinel, the tutor of young Louis XIII who introduced novel methods of teaching. The art of dressage was perfected by the school in Versailles, and under the reign of Louis XV, François Robichon de La Guérinière published his *École de cavalerie (School of Cavalry)* in 1733, a monument of equestrian literature, which brought a new level of sophistication to classical equitation.

The French Revolution destroyed the academy of Versailles, which had served as a model for others schools in Europe. Classical dressage was then denounced as a superfluous luxury by the military and certain civilians who supported Comte d'Aure, an advocate of a "natural" riding style. The horse was no longer used for war. The army took over the art of riding and established the Cadre Noir in Saumur. It was left to the Spanish Riding School in Vienna to safeguard the classical art of riding in its most elevated form, such as it had been created by the masters of the eighteenth century.

This white Lipizzaner horse, which riders around the world admire, carries four centuries of history on its back.

RIGHT: *In front of the judges in the Imperial Hofburg ring, the riders pay homage to Emperor Charles VI, who founded the famous Spanish Riding School of Vienna "with the goal of teaching young noblemen and of training horses in academic equitation."*

At seven o'clock in the morning the pale light gradually reveals the ring in the Winter Riding School in Hofburg, the imperial palace in Vienna. Everything is white and majestic: the walls, the galleries that support forty-six Corinthian columns, the luster of crystal . . . the silence of a deserted cathedral.

A double door opens. Eight white stallions appear, manes flowing, reserved, elegant. The atmosphere commands reverence, veneration. The riders in coffee brown tailcoats, white pants, and gloves lead them at a walk into the ring; slowly, very slowly, almost without moving, they face the former imperial box where a portrait of Charles VI is displayed. Moving their right arms toward their golden braided bicornes, they doff their hats. With a formal bow, they pay homage to the emperor, their protector, and the founder of the Winter Riding School, the most beautiful school in the world. The *Morgenarbeit*, or morning work, can begin. Each rider will respect this ritual every day of his equestrian life, as his predecessors have done for four hundred years. This daily training is in preparation for a magnificent ballet. The Spanish Riding School of Vienna is the oldest institute where the classic art of riding is still practiced today in its purest form. "The artist is personified by the trainer, and the horse is material to mold. Together, they represent a sort of masterpiece, which is moreover ephemeral, discernible only in the movement itself," explains Colonel Hans Handler, former director of the prestigious school.

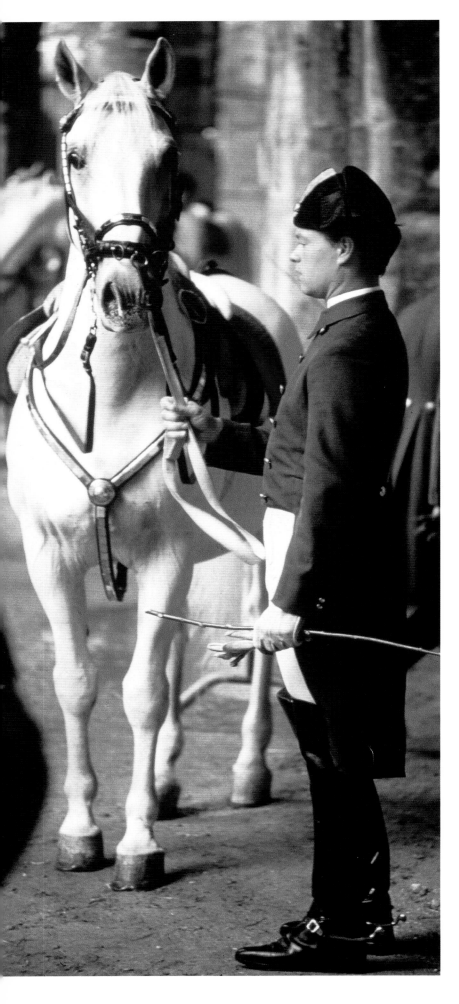

Your nobility is palpable, even in the hand of the cavalier who, through his noble thoughts, brings you with profound feelings toward a world that lies between myth and mystery....

ANGEL PERALTA
Spanish writer and poet, bull breeder
and rejoneador (born in 1926).
Excerpt from the poem, "My Companion"

*The discrete elegance of the uniform
and the simple birch wood crop
symbolize the dignity that befits
riders from the Spanish Riding
School of Vienna.*

On the soft track, riders and horses move along the walls, separate, cut across in front of each other, and trace perfect circles that recross each other. First limbering up with a walk, then a trot, gently, rhythmically. On the bit, their impatience under control, the broad-backed, muscular stallions go into a slow, collected canter. Each stride is exact, controlled. Their backs are supple and their eyes intent, dark, and unfathomable, eyes that reflect intense concentration.

At first glance, the uninitiated spectator might imagine that he is witnessing a parody of the past, an esoteric, gratuitous performance. But in this quasi-religious silence is the muffled hammering of hooves, the quiet murmurs of the riders, the regular breathing of these vibrant horses. The simple birchwood pole and the spare elegance of the uniform symbolize the dignity, which suits the rider. His heritage is the glory that Vienna had known in the past. "We are the link in a long chain of men who pass down treasure through generations of grateful hands. It's our duty to preserve this heritage and to ensure that it will be passed down intact to the generations to come," says Colonel Handler.

The classical school defines only one way to make progress: in order, discipline, and respect for unchanging principles. Every day there are the same exercises, the same efforts, and the same difficulties to overcome. From the age of three and a half, the young stallion trains in the ring. Its training follows a slow, systematic progression, which prepares it physically and mentally to attain perfect equilibrium before the performance. Only the best horses

The stallion that performs the capriole, a classical jump, must keep his tail braided so that his hair remains in place when he kicks his hind legs.

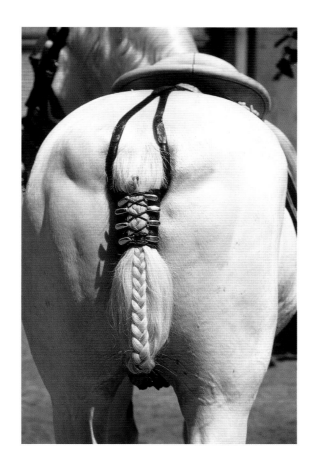

Close to the Winter Riding School, in the heart of Stalburg, there's a Renaissance palace built originally for Emperor Maximilian II. It is here that the Lipizaners from the Spanish Riding School of Vienna are kept.

One of the high points of dressage involves working with long reins, during which the stallion performs steps and figures of the classical school, which he learned from his rider.

receive this assignment to endure long years in the constant search for perfection. It is said that no other single method allows the horses to flourish in classical equitation.

Here riding is a science, "an art continually unfinished," say numerous partisans. An alliance between two beings, the goal of which is not to obtain a victory but a mutual understanding. It's the myth of the centaur that has been celebrated continuously, every day in this same place for centuries by generations of riders. In this temple of knowledge, human errors are suppressed, prejudices and preconceived ideas put aside. The Spanish Riding School of Vienna is without a doubt "an island of timelessness," evidence preserved in history. Imperial Vienna is the same, at least for those who discover it. The city continues to have its monuments restored, to maintain its teahouses with the wainscoting of the eighteenth century, to unearth the remnants of its glorious past, from the antiquated side of a city where life seems to have stopped a century before, on a night in November 1918. The Hapsburg Empire vanished like a dream. Its capital, constantly evolving, imposing, and eternal, suddenly seemed too grand for tiny little Austria. Vienna is the very image of the waltz: by turns, stiff and graceful, calm and intoxicating, prudish and unsettling. The collection of mirrors at the Schönbrunn Palace, the famous Prater wheel, the twirling of a Strauss waltz, the courtly balls at the opera, all of these symbols, so well known, make up the fabric of the Spanish Riding School of Vienna.

The first known document valuing a *manège espagnol* dates from 1572. In that time period when "horse ballets" were in fashion an open-air carousel stood on the site of the present-day Josefplatz, in the former imperial gardens and close to the palace. On May 19, 1580, Archduke Karl, son of the emperor, Ferdinand I, founded the royal stud farm in the small village of Lipizza. There they would proceed "to breed the best horses destined for the imperial court, that is to say, those who will be chosen every time; they will be the strongest to be found anywhere."

Lipizza is located in the Karst, in northwest Slovenia. A region of sparse vegetation, battered by winds, bristling with rocks, but known since antiquity for breeding horses. The soil was cleared of rocks and covered little by little with forests and meadows to welcome nine stallions and twenty-four mares imported from Spain for the Hapsburg Empire. Löhneyssen, praised the Andalusian horses in this way: "They are the most intelligent, the most daring, the most generous . . . and in the ring, the most docile." They will create a lineage there, and Lipizza will give them the name that they will always carry: the Lipizzaners.

RIGHT: *The "dance of the white stallions," reminiscent of carousels from the past, require maximum concentration and precision.*

BELOW: *In all its magnificence, the "capriole" requires the highest level of dressage.*

The gods have given man the ability to teach a sense of duty to his peers through the spoken word, but it is clear that the horse cannot be taught anything through the spoken word.

XENOPHON
Greek writer, philosopher and politician (circa 430 B.C.–355 B.C.)
Excerpt from the book *On the Art of Horsemanship*

Neither wars, nor earthquakes, nor fires, nor even the equine plague could undermine the nobility of these white horses, which the whole world admires. However, in May of 1915, all of the stallions, brood mares, and foals were evacuated from Lipizza and distributed between Laxenberg, near Vienna, and Kladrub in Bohemia. After the collapse of the Austro-Hungarian Empire, it took two years of negotiations between Italy and Austria, each country fighting for its rights over the Lipizza stud farm, to find a solution to the conflict, which was to divide up the horses. That's how the new Lipizzan homeland in Vienna became the Stud Piber, in the Austrian province of Styria. A haven of peace reigned over almost fifteen hundred acres of high mountain pasture. And because this exceptional breed demands it, the selection of horses is always conducted with scientific precision: only the stallions that have demonstrated extraordinary qualities at the time of their training at the Spanish Riding School have the right to pass on their heredity. And their coats must still be spotless at ten years of age, according to an imperial decree from the nineteenth century. This is because the prince of horses is born with a black, gray, or brown coat, which becomes progressively lighter as the years pass.

The Lipizzaners emerge, one after the other, in the order of their stall accommodations in the "Stallburg," the oldest wing of the Hofburg, in the Renaissance Palace. They are brushed and harnessed. Each horse jumps over the gate in turn. Traffic stops for a few moments to allow the procession to pass by. Then the horses' shoes ring out on the hundred-year-old paving stones, which lead to the winter

Be sure not to bother her if at all possible; it may smother her kindness for she is to horses what a flower is to a fruit.

ANTOINE DE PLUVINEL
Founder of the first French Academy of Equitation

Until the age of three and a half, the young Lipizzaners frolic in the Austrian stud farms of Piber. After the first selection is made, they're sent to Vienna for training. Their coat is dark at birth but gradually lightens. It turns white between the ages of seven and ten.

Since 1920, the Stud Piber has been the exclusive provider for the Riding School of Vienna, but, the Lipizza Stud Farm in Slovenia is the birthplace of Lipizzaners. The farm is a green oasis, a plantation of oaks, maples and linden trees.

ring. This happens every three-quarters of an hour for each of the groups that come, one after the other, until the thirteen strokes of the church bells of Saint Michael's have sounded.

Every year, hundreds of thousands of visitors attend these trials with the Viennese riders. It isn't easy to obtain a ticket for the famous "dance of the white stallions," which takes place twice a week in the evening. Those who succeed never leave unaffected. Faced with the beauty of the performance, some at times have tears in their eyes. Others applaud, quietly, at each feat. Yet others, fewer in number, give the impression that the Spanish School of Vienna is only a charming anachronism, a wonderful source of revenue for the Viennese Office of Tourism. But these people don't know that the Lipizzaners have been trained to execute performances for the imperial court; and this evening again they will dance in the Hofburg ring.

It's seven in the evening. The quiet murmuring of the audience pours out in the Hofburg Winter School, which is bathed in light. The double door opens. Eight riders in coffee brown tailcoats, mounted on white stallions with golden bridles enter to the tune of "L'Arlésienne" by Bizet. They walk slowly, in single file, and face the grandstand. There in a single motion, the men doff their hats and bow to the portrait of Emperor Charles VI. The "dance of the white stallions" can begin.

Birthplace of Stars

IRELAND

Known for its mild climate and rich soil, the county of Kildare

became the birthplace of the stars of the equestrian planet,

a closed world where the Thoroughbred is king.

It's a fairy tale in this Ireland where racing is a passion.

To race horses as a hobby or for pleasure or fame, mounted or harnessed, across the open country or in a ring: this is what men have done for nearly four thousand years. But the homeland of Thoroughbred racing is England. It no doubt owes this fact to the Crusades. It is said that Richard the Lionheart, impassioned by the value of Arabian horses, organized the first race, endowed with three prizes, on Epsom moor. His successor, King John of England (known as John Lackland) set up a royal stable intended for tests of speed. Several racetracks were already in existence by the end of the fifteenth century when James I created a racetrack in Newmarket. From the end of the seventeenth century, the monarchs and the British nobles directed their research toward training a breed devised for speed. The East then gave the West what it was missing: Arabian steeds with their delicate, feline grace.

During the reign of Charles II, sportsmen went to Morocco and Arabia in order to buy stallions to cover the royal mares, meticulously selected to produce horses most gifted for speed. At the beginning of the next century, the descendants of these broodmares were introduced to three stallions that came from the East: Byerley Turk, Goldolphin Arabian, and Darley Arabian. The mixed lineage from these three sires gave England the first champions, among which were the famous Matchem, Herod, and Eclipse. These were the prodigal horses of the eighteenth century; horses that left their mark on all of the great Thoroughbred dynasties throughout the world.

From that point on, the descendants of the English Thoroughbreds were recorded in the General Stud Book. Artists were called on to paint the portraits of the masters and horses who posed together for posterity. With the creation of the Jockey Club in 1750, whose mission was to establish methods for training Thoroughbreds and regulations for racing, the English equestrian sport was off and running. Five of the classic trials that are run today throughout the world date back to these times: Saint Leger, Oaks, Derby, 1000

Guineas, and 2000 Guineas. The logic of the competition demands the most exhaustive selection of Thoroughbreds. Stirrups are kept as short as possible, and the jockey's weight is thrust forward. The heavy saddle has been replaced by a small oval seat.

It was truly a revolution in the world of riding that swept the European continent; first Paris, where the first regular tests of the gallop "English style" took place starting in 1775 on the Plain of Fine Sands, then on the Champs de Mars military esplanade; later Germany, Italy, Poland, North and South America, Japan, New Zealand, South Africa.... From one end of the universe to the other, the nobility had a passion for spirited Thoroughbreds that were built for speed. To own a racing stable represented if not privilege, at least evidence of a high social standing. Whereas the best horses were invited to participate in the most prestigious events, the racetracks were opened to the masses and betting became more democratic.

During the twentieth century, there were hardly any countries that didn't have stud farms, racetracks, and racing. The "world of the gallop" continued to develop a structure: fashionable, impenetrable, with its hierarchy of stable boys, jockeys, and trainers, its great stables, and its owners with prestigious names—Rothschild, Boussac, Agha Khan, emirs from the Gulf, and wealthy Japanese businessmen. But through intermediary bookmakers or organizations like the PMU (Paris mutuel urbain—betting office) in France, and with a very modest stake, the rich and the less rich could henceforth try their luck at the races. Paradoxically, the taste for gambling overrode the appeal of horses. Most of the betters never saw the racehorses they were putting money on. They knew nothing about their relative qualities and relied on tips from newspapers. The success of racing, simultaneously aristocratic and working-class, is the result of a very strange alchemy.

Primarily dedicated to breeding Thoroughbreds, the county of Kildare enjoys a mild and humid climate, lush pastures planted with century-old trees, and soil of exceptional quality. At the beginning of spring, colts from all over the world come to accept the tributes paid to them by great, prize-winning stallions.

Curragh. An autumn morning, the tender grass shining with dew. The air is moist and mild; the earth is green and very lush. It's here on this vast natural grassland three thousand years ago that the Celts raced their horses harnessed to legendary two-wheeled chariots. Since that time the county of Kildare has become, completely on its own, the birthplace of the stars of the equestrian planet: the Thoroughbreds. Here, on the landscape of vast spaces of a deep, pure, green, the most beautiful stud farms in the world sparkle. It is peaceful and calm, the meadows are beautifully kept with trimmed hedges, and trails are bordered with white lilies.

It is a closed world, secret and protected. Everywhere, high, stone walls, imposing gates, and a bank of cameras keep watch. Isolated in their paddocks with acres of freedom, several silhouettes, with manes flowing and elegant, slender legs, dot the pastures. The mares are near their colts, the offspring that will soon make the financial market tremble. And further away, the stallions, idle sultans, kings whose temperament and desire are perpetuated in the great dynasties of Thoroughbreds. Here, in a serene, well-managed setting they make champions, stars, shining heroes of racetracks around the world. It is said that the county of Kildare benefits, "from a chalk-rich soil that causes the land to have sweet-smelling pastures, good for giving horses a strong bone structure . . . and a moist, mild climate which is better for growing oats than wheat." The mysteries of the soil are

Birthplace of Stars: IRELAND

Cloaked in ebony, fire, ivory, and honey,
The manes wave the flags of endurance …
A single horse conquers an oat-filled illusion,
A simple compensation for a tomorrow that demands
a thousand new labors.

CHRYSTELLE GASNE-COTELLE
French writer, born in 1954
From the poem "L'écheveau en Bataille" (The Snarled Battle)

It has been proven, that along with climate, soil is of the utmost importance when breeding Thoroughbreds. Due to these natural assets, this soil of Ireland was able to develop a breeding tradition, a tradition rooted in the innate ability of many of the Irish to understand horses. The ponies of Connemara, skilled at fox hunting, and Irish draft horses useful for farm work, were part of the landscape and of people's everyday lives. The Thoroughbred is a "divine creature that appeared suddenly like a gift from God," a fairy tale in "the land of heart's desire" from the poet William Butler Yeats.

The story begins with Colonel William Hall Walker, in an Ireland from a different time, isolated and wild, genuine. Son of a Scottish brewer, he bought a farm in Tully, in 1902, near the village of Kildare, and then set about breeding English Thoroughbreds. At that time he had stables built with skylights, so that the transparency allowed the light from the stars could shine through: Hall Walker believed in the influence of the stars on living things in general, and on horses in particular. That is how the great winners of the seven popular classic races came into being during that century in England. Without a doubt it was the greatest honor paid to methods of breeding and to the colonel's small farm, which was labeled as eccentric, irrational, and inspired. Then, in 1943, the Tully property was handed over to the Irish government which brought it to the level of a national stud farm. Simultaneously, Son Altesse Agha Khan, spiritual leader of the Ismali, with whom Colonel Walker had shared his passion and his knowledge, got involved in the breeding of Thoroughbreds in Ireland. His first magnificent stud farms came into being in Kildare. For half a century he cherished the Thoroughbreds that raced under his colors.

In 1975, John Magnier, originally from the county of Cork, founded Coolmore Stud, which became one of the greatest stud farms in the world, and without a doubt, the most successful in our time: operating room, pool, foaling stall under video surveillance, and nursery with a two-way mirror for the newborns. Each foal may potentially be a future champion.

During the spring, Coolmore with its six thousand acres of grassland will welcome nearly seven hundred mares. They will come here from England, France, Italy, Japan, and the United States, to accept the tributes paid to them by great, prize-winning stallions. The "emperors of stallions" live in this lap of luxury, where the cost of covering a mare runs into hundreds of thousands of dollars. Among them is the highly venerated Peintre Célèbre who won the Arc de Triomphe prize by five lengths at the age of three—and

Thoroughbreds, lively and sensitive by nature and bred for speed, rival each other in elegance. They are slender and supple, with delicate heads and straight profiles, long necks, and a low and extended stride.

whose happy owners pocketed more than one million dollars during the year. By his side, the magnificent Desert King, winner of the Irish Derby, the brilliant Sadler's Wells, sire of a great lineage, and so many other Thoroughbred legends.

Several white fences down the road from Coolmore is Kildangan Stud, one of the five Irish stud farms of the sheik Mohammed Bin Rashid al-Maktoum. The gate opens majestically on well-ordered grasslands and hundred-year-old oak trees. Quiet, spacious, serene, muffled activity. . . . The central path leads straight to a sleepy country house, a magnificent building built in the Kentucky style of architecture from the turn of the century, all red brick with a slate roof, which will be visible when the blades of the helicopter announce the arrival of the prince and his entourage. The rest of the time the stallions and the mares reign supreme. Their property: fifteen hundred acres of grassland and seven stables connected by tracks of soft, raked sand,

The foal gallops for the first time in the field with its mother. It begins training at eighteen months and can begin to run in its second year. At age four a champion is at the end of its racing days. It then returns to the farm as a stallion.

A true athlete, a Thoroughbred runs a kilometer, from start to finish, in less than fifty-six seconds. So as not to work against the horse and in order to encourage its speed, the jockey stands in very short stirrups over the horse.

surrounded by trimmed hedges. No less than seventy people are at their disposal: walking the horses, providing meals, "treats," and warm baths, and brushing their coats until they shine.

In Kildangan, there is the right way to approach perfection. Even the cows contribute to the well-being of the Thoroughbreds, by keeping them company in the paddocks, grazing on the grass, which keeps it at an ideal height! It is the price that the Sheik of Dubai is prepared to pay, in order to mold his future champion, the one like Singerspeil several years ago who will make his colors blaze at the Dubai World Cup, the racetrack with the richest purse in the world at six million dollars!

Around thirty private stud farms participated in the rapid development of the "island of Celts and fairies," and in this way, came to place first in the European ranking of thoroughbred breeding. With two hundred fifty days of racing per year, and twenty-seven racetracks, the equestrian sector, which employs directly or indirectly more than fifty thousand people in the country, handles large sums of money, exempt from taxes for a dozen years.

Going to the racetrack in Ireland is much more than a simple outing. Many families plan their vacations around the most important events.

Standing in their seats, among family or friends, each fan dives without restraint into the spirit of the race, betting on his favorite until it crosses the finish line.

Nearly 1,400 races take place every year in Ireland between mid-March and November. Typically, the distance measures 2,400 meters, over which a sprinter can attain a speed of about seventy kilometers an hour.

There are no words to describe the feelings that Thorough-bred racing arouses in Ireland. More than a simple sport, more than entertainment, racing is a passion. Gambling, betting, business, the victory party . . . memories of Curragh, memories of Leopold town! Who will make racing his career? Who will be the star of the year?

All of the villages, even the most secluded, have their bookmakers. In the afternoon, men and women come and go. Sometimes with a very modest stake, each one comes to try his luck, to take time to relax before meeting at the pub. There, words pour out, rhythmically due to the ceremony of drinking and fiddle tunes. But the Irish dive into the race-track, betting on their favorite, which they encourage with-out restraint, until the hallowed area of the winner's circle.

Many families plan their vacations according to the most important events. First the five classics in Curragh, then the

They run outstretched, neither rising up nor rushing ahead, and they look like wooden horses that, fully extended, might be joined to the edge of a large horizontal circle, moving around an axis at the greatest speed imaginable.

PIERRE JEAN GROSLEY,
London

*Because it is frank, swift, and strong,
the authentic English horse is comparable
to the greatest steed in the world.*

GERVAE MARKHAM

*Far from the track, crowd, and flood-
lights, the lad, or stable-boy cares for,
feeds, pampers, and watches over the
athlete. With all his know-how and
familiarity of horses, with all the
boundless love that he has for them,
he is undoubtedly the most important
person in the thoroughbred's life and
in cultivating champions.*

derbies in Leopardstown, Fairyhouse or Punchestown, which all of high society attends, the ladies competing for original hat designs. Then come the epic races, which take place over several days, at Galway, Trale, Listowel, and the famous "2000" of Laytown, the only official event that takes place on a beach, where the date is determined in August by the tide!

One of the most highly attended equestrian events takes place the day after Christmas, near Dublin, over four days during which the racetrack in Leopardstown is never empty. The National Hunt, an obstacle course, is by far the most popular of the races. This comes as no surprise since racing over fences started in Ireland in 1752 to settle a differ-ence between two gentlemanfarmers. Riding at top speed across fields, on their horses, jumping ditches, sunken lanes, hedges, and low walls, they traveled four and a half miles between the Buttevant and Doneraile churches. And so the steeplechase was born. The very first event of this kind took place in England, in March 1837, as the Liverpool Grand National, before spreading out over five continents. Today, most of the Thoroughbreds that race in England are born in Ireland and are trained there. The two nations understand each other on this point: the love of horses and of racing.

The Cowboys of the Twenty-first Century

CANADA

Skilled riders, the cowboys of western Canada are only distant

cousins to the mythical adventurers of the Hollywood Western.

Their knowledge is practical, ancestral. Calgary, city of

the future, has not forgotten the pioneers who created it.

The first immigrants—explorers, hunters, or trappers—played the most heroic role in the conquest of the American West. They were often on horseback, spoke the Indian dialects, and were shrewd and experienced like the trackers. They wrote a page in history about adventure and bravery for which this new continent is proud. Then, in the nineteenth century, the immense and untouched lands from Texas to Canada began breeding livestock that proliferated. This marked a great moment in American history.

In 1875, the great Texas plains, covered with thorny holm oak, were home to some five million longhorns, large cattle whose horns could attain one and a half feet in length—descendants of the cattle brought to Mexico by the conquistadors. Hundreds of men mounted on cowponies, moved the cattle north into the Great Plains in search of grasslands and markets.

First they aimed for the closest market, Louisiana; then they marked the cattle with an iron or a notch in the ear, and drove them towards Missouri, St. Louis, Chicago. It was for this rough, dangerous work that they used horses.

The new centaurs were Texas horsemen who, did not hesitate to confront the vast plains of the American West. They drove thousands of animals before them and opened up trails. The cowboy era was born. The men were of all ages, but mostly young, many of them veterans of the Civil War. More than half a million cattle came up from the south each year, and ranches multiplied. Each one had its brand duly registered by the local authorities and stamped with a hot iron on the animal's flanks. Once a year, the cowboys rounded up the great herds so that each owner could take his share.

In less than twenty years the influx of pioneers signaled the

Men are better when riding, more just and more understanding, and more alert and more at ease and more under-taking, and better knowing of all countries and all passages…

EDWARD, DUKE OF YORK

end of these legendary migrations. Everywhere the barbed wire fencing began to define the properties. Although the open land was supposed to belong to ranchers who had access to water, innumerable conflicts resulted in stolen cattle and doctored brands. No longer finding work driving cattle, the cowboy became a ranch hand. During the long months of summer, he lived alone at one of the surveillance posts. His role was limited to taking care of the cattle and mending the fences. During the winter he was temporarily out of work, which forced him to go door to door, doing menial jobs in exchange for room and board.

Thankless jobs devoted to animals and loneliness: this is what filled the rigorous life of the cowboys at the beginning of the twentieth century. Even today the modern cowboy is ready to sit astride a horse for a week, in any

kind of weather and make his way back to town, where meager wages are spent on saloons, alcohol, and girls. Each spring, comes the time to round up and break in the young horses, and each man is proud to demonstrate his talent. Over the years their everyday chores have developed into athletic competition: lassoing bulls and wild horses, bronco-busting, horse racing . . . This is how the rodeo developed from the roundup.

These tough, lonely riders of the wide open spaces are only the distant cousins of the mythical adventurers of the Hollywood Western. The movie business, however, feeds on deception. The cowboy's knowledge is practical and ancestral, made from the legacy of the past. It's with this symbol of freedom that fits him like a glove, that he walks straight into the third millennium.

*Each year in July, the city of
Calgary lives for the stampede,
the famous rodeo founded in 1912.
Cowboys and aficionados gather
by the thousands wearing ten-
gallon hats, silver buckles, and
elaborate boots. Elegant to the
last detail, like the crop of a
woman riding sidesaddle (above).*

Where does western
Canada begin? Almost two thousand miles from Quebec,
in the heart of the prairies of Saskatchewan and Alberta,
which fantasy-filled minds can't imagine without cowboys.
No territory in the world can overcome as dazzling a destiny
as that of western Canada.

Barely two centuries ago, when the Blackfeet or Sihasapa
Indians were still hunting bison, a handful of trappers
ventured to Quebec looking for furs, guided by the navigable
rivers into extensive, unknown territory. Today oil flows
there like water, silos of wheat rise up like cathedrals, horses
and livestock graze by the thousands. And the cities of the
west rival their great sister cities on the European continent,
opening wide their arms to all the world's urbanity.

Welcome to these urban expansions that only happen
west of the Atlantic. Welcome to the new pioneers and their
insatiable spirit of enterprise. Calgary, formerly known as
the "cow town," has mushroomed. It provides glass and
steel skyscrapers where the cowboys now get around in
elevators, like the oil tycoons. In the stockyards on 21st
Avenue, there are thousands of cattle from all of the ranches
south of Alberta, on their way to auction. In the neighboring
skyscrapers, businessmen speculate on the price per barrel
of oil. Each street, each square, each neighborhood displays
"western style" in its windows, its neo-Victorian memorial,
its pioneer museum, the mounted police, or the ancestors of
the prairie, the Indians.

The chuck wagon race, lively and animated, dates back to when western pioneers tried to flee Indian attacks in their covered wagons.

The men and women of Calgary—gentleman farmers, cowboys, cowgirls, or businesspeople—cross the avenues and the hanging gardens, sporting white Stetsons, silver belt buckles, and cowboy boots. During the transitional season between winter and summer, when nature explodes in less than two weeks, everyone without exception is seized by an irresistible desire to stroll outdoors and to cook barbecue by a log cabin. During the month of July, Calgary is operating on "stampede" time, described as "the biggest outdoor show in the world."

"Stampede?" It's a word used in the American West to designate the unstoppable motion of a herd of animals running as if crazy and blind, when they jostle and trample each other to death. A stampede can start with a rifle shot, an electrical storm, or the odor of water smelled from several miles away. "Nothing can stop a stampede," recall the cowboys who left the vast prairies of rich grassland to come cheer the rodeo stars during the Calgary Stampede, ten days of the Far West celebration. Their forefathers, the cowboys of the great migrations, who created this event in 1886, at the time of the first cattle fair in Calgary. Having driven their herds to the center of the city, they organized, for their enjoyment, benefit competitions in lassoing and riding. Twenty-six years later, Guy Weadick, a public entertainer who enjoyed roping, made official this gathering of champion ropers and riders. This colorful exhibition, evidence of the affection this Western city has for the pioneers who settled it, soon became the major event in western Canada.

An impressive parade through the streets of Calgary opens the stampede. This is the occasion for the Canadian Royal Gendarmerie to pay homage to the mounted police who, in the past, patrolled the Canadian West to keep the peace.

To stay on an unbroken horse (bronco) for eight seconds, with or without a saddle, is a challenge that professional cowboys across America all take in their battle for the top prizes at Calgary.

Calgary is celebrating. Cowboys have come from all over the continent; even the airport waiting room is bathed in country music and Western decor; the hostesses wear jeans, plaid shirts, and neckerchiefs. Aficionados arrive from the four corners of Canada, the United States, and sometimes Europe, to join with the population, which jumps from eight hundred thousand to two million inhabitants. There are already hundreds of celebrants dancing and singing in the middle of the street, wearing ten-gallon hats. Everyone imagines himself in the place of those who long ago went beyond the limits of the old Wild West. And each new arrival plays the game, even if he has never sat astride except on a barstool.

On the steps of the immense Stampede Park stadium, where the roof is shaped like a horse's saddle, is a colorfully dressed crowd, day and night, and a collection of odors: those from the nearby stables, and those of sweet and sour chicken, hamburger, and cinnamon doughnuts. In the paddocks, more than a thousand horses nervously wait their turns. And in the ring, the best professionals in the world compete for a half-million dollar purse! The famous "Half Million Dollar Rodeo" offers $500,000.00, the highest prize in the history of the sport.

In the past a champion might have found himself rewarded with a horse, a saddle, or a tidy little sum that allowed him to supplement his meager salary as a cowboy. Times change: the West has changed its look and the rodeo is a full-time job. In order to enroll in one or another of these competitive events, the cowboys must have achieved a maximum number of points in rodeos held during the year. During the season, from June to September, some participate in three or four rodeos each day! There are more than six hundred official rodeos each year in North America and each attracts more spectators than a football or baseball game. The reason for this huge success is that behind this show, this movement, this folklore, lies a great tradition and a deep-rooted love of horses. Each has its rules and its trophies, and all demand a high degree of skill and athletic ability: riding a wild horse or bronco, with or without a saddle (bronco riding), catching a steer by the horns (steer wrestling), lassoing a calf (calf roping), and staying on a bull weighing almost two

thousand pounds (bull riding). It would take an entire book to describe all of them.

Every evening, the highlight of the show is reserved for another category of adventurers, those who take off on the wild chuckwagon race. Long ago, these wagons, pulled by horses, provided the supplies for the cowboys during the cattle drive. Four teams fight for victory. On the starting line are sixteen horses, four to a team. At the bell, the cowboys pounce on a box, symbolizing a stove that they load into the covered wagon before jumping aboard. A cloud of dust and the crowd goes wild. One minute fifteen seconds in the limelight and then it's over. Except for the winner. Because after nine days of elimination trials comes the long-awaited, magnificent finale when the first prize goes up to fifty thousand dollars! As the festival program states, "the champion risks his life each time."

In the Canadian West, the Calgary Stampede is easily the best way to become a hero, but rarely the way to become rich. Countless ranches, towns, and cities set up rodeos where boys and girls get their start, before dreaming, one day maybe, to compete in a national division. But the life of a cowboy is not only for sport or for show. To find out this first truth it is necessary to go to the vast prairies of Alberta. There, all the way to the horizon, sheared by the Rocky Mountain peaks, nearly four million horses and cattle share the space and the light of these immense lands reserved for breeding. Herds to watch over, to move from one pasture to another, to brand, to take care of, and, at the end of the season, to sort into different groups according

to sales made by the owner. The use of pickup trucks, live-stock trucks, planes, or helicopters to ride herd of animals heralded the end of the myth of the Far West. But not a single breeder knew how to survive without the services of the cowboys.

   While dawn pierced through the horizon on the Prairie, Rocky Hill, who was around fifty and weathered by the sun, commented on his life as a free man, while poking the fire under an old, dented coffeemaker that was percolating. He was born in the prairie of an Indian mother and a European father. All of his life, he drove herds and took care of horses and longhorns, going from one ranch to another each spring. Today he is the only wage earner on a ranch extending hundreds of acres. His work is to oversee several hundred heads of half-wild livestock, with the goal of fattening them up before taking them to slaughter. But more than anything else, Rocky Hill is here to care for and train approximately one hundred Quarter Horses and Morgans; horses that are actors, extras, and stunt horses for the movies. He remembers having gotten them ready for

There's no rest during winter for
a cowboy. In the snow and wind,
he stays astride his horse, making
sure watering places have not
frozen over. He tends to, cares for,
and feeds his herds.

Otto Preminger's *River of No Return* with Marilyn Monroe,
in 1995, *Eaters of the Dead* in 1997 . . . The Canadian West has
been one of the greatest cinematic centers on the entire
continent. Certainly its fame has never attained that of its
American equivalent. Is it because it lacks a Hollywood to
popularize its image?

"By living here, I have the feeling that society doesn't take
away my independence," explains Rocky, the cowboy who
doesn't wait for sunrise to get in the saddle, on a Quarter
Horse, his companion in the solitude. All around, there's a
sea of grass waves in the cocoon-like fog of the early morning. Perhaps, as the pair grows distant, then slowly disappears toward the horizon, slowly, like a single being, you
can imagine the feeling of freedom the man experiences
astride a horse, in the sun, the rain, the snow, in the dust
or the *chinook*, the hot, dry wind that makes waves appear
suddenly on the high grassy prairie. When it's time for the
spring roundup, Rock Hill calls on seasonal cowboys for
help in order to carry out the counting and branding of the
longhorns, and the castration of calves. But he knows that
the applicants won't be rushing, because the life is rough
and lonely, and the wages are low—between four hundred
and six hundred dollars a month, plus room and board, for
an exhausting job that goes from dawn until dusk, seven
days a week, with little time to sit by the fire and drink a
beer and try to solve the world's problems.

For several years now, different ways of using a horse
have made the life of a modern cowboy more appealing.
Remembering the long trails that their ancestors followed,
some cowboys ride trails in the Rocky Mountains, which
brings together riders from faraway countries. Others

When pick-ups, cattle trucks, motorbikes and planes came onto the scene to transport and oversee livestock, it was thought that the mythical Far West would come to an end. But as long as there are men who share their solitude with a horse, the legend will live on.

devote themselves to taming and training saddle horses according to methods based on gentleness and understanding, very far from the old school, which "borke" a horse in five days.

The heritage of the West is no longer confined to ranches. Western horseback riding, which requires balance, fluidity, and agility, holds a considerable attraction for riders of all social classes and experiences. In this still Wild West, where history and its treasures were passed along from one generation to the next, eager for progress, the cowboy knows how to combine the past and the present.

The Steeds of the Sahara

TUNISIA

In the steppes of southern Tunisia, horses are extraordinary beings. Ridden for hunting or racing, these purebred Arabians attest to the tradition of ancient nomads.

Four thousand years ago, the Near East discovered the horse and made it famous. At first, this noble animal from Asia Minor and western Syria was rare, and exotic; it was kept by princes or harnessed to a royal chariot. Eventually, the horse assisted aristocrats in hunting and war. When the Indo-European peoples arrived in the eastern Mediterranean, especially the Hittites on their two-wheeled chariots, the region underwent major changes in terms of military art and hunting in open country. Soon the draft horse had a rider—*pithallu*, a term designating a cavalier and his horse who walked alongside the carts. As recorded in Assyrian bas-reliefs, men didn't ride bareback but used a kind of blanket on the horse, perhaps an animal hide. They were most likely messengers, scouts, or hunters. Most of the horses used by the Babylonians and Assyrians came from mountainous regions inhabited by the Kassites and Hurrites. A figurine found in Marlik, dating back to the end of the second millennium B.C.E, attests to the first saddle in these areas. It had a rim both in front and back meant to support the rider. To the west, in Palestine and Phoenicia, the Egyptians were the ones who provided horses to regional armies, including King Solomon's army. Because the kingdom of the pharoahs was so dry, breeding was practiced in territories like Nubia, which had a more moderate climate. Meanwhile, in Mesopotamia, there emerged the winged horse, the symbol of the celestial world, the prototype of Pegasus. This would become the hero of the most beautiful tale of the *Arabian Nights* and would live a long time on the walls of Teheran.

The Near East takes pride in its horse, elegant, slender, high-strung, and capable of great speed—nature's most beautiful creation, many say. Above all, the Arabian is very carefully bred. The Prophet loves horses; he encourages the entire Muslim world to breed and expand its equine bloodstock as they are warhorses for the messengers of Islam. To this end, horse racing was developed,

Oh you, Lord of the Air,
Great Drinker of clouds,
Smoke of hookah,
Guide the riders of the wind
Into the desert's Arabian Nights.

JEAN MARCILLY
French writer and international reporter.
Poetic prologue "Légende d'Orient" in the book
entitled *Gilbert Michaud*, Rosentiel's London, 1996

both short-distance races for young horses and long races, allowing breeders to refine their selection. The prizes awarded to the owners of the winners were exclusively devoted to promote breeding.

The Arabs created a strong horse that was supple, not demanding, fit for long journeys in arid lands. Their military strength grew considerably as the prophet Mohammed unified tribes. The result was astounding: the cavaliers of Islam galloped into Persia, Egypt, and Libya. As early as the end of the seventh century, they erupted into the Maghreb before taking Spain. It wasn't until they reached Poitiers, in the heart of France, that the Arab cavalry came up against a wall they could not cross.

Because the Prophet called the war holy, the caliphs drew on an unending reserve of men and horses. Among them was Haroun Al-Rachid, Abbasid caliph, whose empire extended from the Atlantic to Chinese Turkmen-

istan, from India to the Black Sea. Because of his passion for horse racing, he owned huge stables, hunted, and hosted parties in which competitors indulged in all kinds of equestrian contests, including archery astride a galloping mount. Haroun Al-Rachid, who was the first caliph to play polo, made the sport popular among all social classes.

The Arabian horse is spirited, tough, fierce, and clever like its rider. It has crossed every frontier and entered every continent. Poets have celebrated it ceaselessly. Because it is able to pass its characteristics along to its offspring, the Arabian has created new breeds or participated in improving old ones. For the Arab peoples, the Arabian horse is a symbol of divine inspiration. Integral to the Islamic religion, rooted in its tradition and even their soul, the lord of horses will forever be a friend to care for, protect, and love.

According to specialists, it's in the region of Maknassi that the most typical Tunisian purebreds are born today. Pampered like children, the horses lead their lives close to their original birthplace. Some make their mark on the racetrack, others in long distance events.

"The goods of this world, until the day of the last judgment, shall hang from the hair between the eyes of our horses. . . ." This legend recounted by the horsemen of Maknassi, a village in southern Tunisia, is popular in the Sahara, and the words of the Prophet on which it is based are an article of faith. "Love horses, care for them, they deserve your tenderness: treat them like your children, feed them like friends and clothe them with care! For the love of Allah, do not neglect yourself for you shall repent of it in this house as in the next one." If you talk to a breeder of purebred Arabians, he will tell you: "If you ride horses, abandon greyhounds, and if your buckles jingle, verses will leave your head."

When you speak with a trainer of these noble horse, one who knows about the ancient nomads, he will talk to you about the young horse's fiery quality, its beauty, and the importance of training; and he will pronounce this well-known adage: "Feed a one-year-old colt well and sprains will be avoided. Ride it when it is two or three, until it is submissive. Feed it well between the ages of three and four. Then ride it again forever after."

Forced by the advancing desert sand and pastures disappearing into the distance, the cavaliers of the Sahara had to cross the salty lakes and then the mountains, behind which lay the vast steppes. The mountains are tawny, a kind of Saharan ochre. In the foothills, the cavalier pitched their horsehair tents, eventually building low, stone houses like

fortresses. Then they plowed the earth to grow barley and
olive trees. Today, they lead sedentary lives and camels are
no longer part of their herds. But no one has lost their atavis-
tic love of the horse, especially their own horses, without
which life would be inconceivable. And yet this noble
animal puts a serious strain on the family budget.

And so was born the village of Maknassi, which, in 1911,
captivated a Frenchman by the name of Frédéric Lovy, a
doctor of medicine and a lover of Arabian horses. He settled
there immediately and founded a breeding farm, for which
he brought in purebred stallions from Syria and Egypt. A
fervent champion of racing purebred Arabians, he refused to
allow English half-breds to participate. Many of his horses
raced in Kassar Saïd, the Tunis racetrack. His success was
epitomized by Damas who won twenty-nine out of thirty-
one races and was second in the other two. But in 1956, the
year Tunisia won its independence, Dr. Lory had to leave
everything behind: his land, stables, and horses. And so the
riders of Maknassi took over this exceptional breeding farm,
determined to preserve the purity of the race and the methods passed down by their nomad ancestors.

The horse of the Sahara used to be a comrade-in-arms, a
friend of the head of the tent and a servant to the family.
Today, the horse lives in the courtyard of his master's house,
tied to an olive tree, or stands free under a roof of branches.
Women and children will play with the horse, spoiling it
with milk and dates. And the men rest by his side, half
asleep on a mat, staring out into the distance, sipping black,
bitter tea, sweetened like a liqueur. It is during these chats
that the elders pass down their knowledge: they talk about
religion, conflict, love, and, of course, horses; they describe
their ways and their needs, they glorify horses in song and
praise them in poems; they share the remedies that soothe

The love that the riders of the steppes have for purebred racing and hunting with greyhounds points to the aristocracy of the customs of the ancient lords of the Sahara.

Horses are eagles mounted by cavaliers; as long as lances, they arrive piercing the air like a falcon falling down on its prey.

ARAB POEM

and cure horses of sickness, a traditional lore from which many Western veterinarians have learned much.

These men are tireless with words, but they also savor silence. They spend entire days on their horses, devouring the plains, taking the mountains in their stride. " Purebred Arabians grow in beauty under the saddle as they travel," explains Ghobber Ridha, breeder of these noble steeds, which he cares for like sons. The only other animal for which man has such great esteem and respect is the Persian greyhound, "which doesn't eat out of a dirty plate and doesn't drink milk touched by hands." These two passions point to the aristocracy of the customs of the people of Maknassi, to their tastes that have been passed down from the ancient lords of the Sahara.

The Persian greyhounds accompany their master on his visits and they enjoy hospitality, as he does, receiving a part of every dish. But hunting is the supreme joy, for the greyhound can capture a hare in flight. It is said that when

*In the Sahara, the horse is the most beautiful creature
after man: the most noble occupation belongs to
the breeder, the most precious pastime is riding,
and the best domestic act is to care for it.*

GENERAL E. DAUMAS
General Melchior-Jospeh-Eugène Daumas,
head of the Algeria Service for the Ministry of War.
Excerpt from *Chevaux au Sahara* (Horses of the Sahara), 1851

he catches sight of his prey cutting a blade of grass, he
seizes it even before it can swallow what is in its mouth.
At daybreak, when Ghobber Ridha mounts his purebred,
the greyhounds lead the way, their bodies extending like
gazelles, their slender noses grazing the ground. The galloping horse follows close behind. They follow the hare in a
wild race, seizing it by the neck, fighting over it until their
master steps down to the ground to cut its throat on the
spot. This is how the rider in the steppes enjoys his favorite
pastime. His ancestors did the same.

"A good horse in the desert has to travel seventy-five to
ninety miles without stopping for five or six days. With two
days of rest and good nourishment, it can start out again.
Because of this treatment, it will attain an extreme speed."
This remark made by General Daumas illustrates an equally
ancient custom that has continuously been practiced for
centuries: horse racing.

Long before the English invented racetracks and betting,
the Arabs were training their purebreds and racing them.
This practice, which preceded Islam, was nevertheless
praised and encouraged by the Prophet. On this subject, the
Arab scholar Bokhari wrote: "The Prophet raced the trained
horses together; he set a distance of seven thousand meters.
for them to cross, making ordinary horses go a thousand
only." The goal was to refine the selection of the Arabian
horse, which was ridden by the messengers of Islam. And
nothing has changed with regard to this: racing thrives more
than ever on Tunisian soil.

If you want to go to war, buy a horse with a white circle on its forehead and with white stockings on all legs except for the right front one.

HADITH OF THE PROPHET

"Purebred Arabians grow in beauty under the saddle," explains Ghobber Ridha, breeder of these steeds. He raises them like his sons and trains them like athletes.

Nearly four hundred official races take place every year at the Tunis and Monastir tracks. They are flat races only, ranging from three-quarters of a mile to two miles in length. The horses that participate are mostly purebreds raised on the fertile plains of the northern region and selected for their speed. To say "horse of the North" is to emphasize the special nature of the "horse of the South." There is no political boundary between the two groups. The difference is climate, the nature of the land, and the heritage of the past, which means that the breeding conditions have nothing in common. Purebred Arabians kept in racing stables, as their English relatives are kept, lose their essential qualities and become weaker. But, in the Sahara, they have silence and wind, space and a boundless horizon. Here in the south, they lead a life that is similar to that of their origin.

The steppe region benefits from a soil that is both soft and firm. The air is dry, pure, and light. The horse lives with its master and drinks only pure water and eats only the best food. Experts believe that it is here, in this special part of the world, that the most typical Tunisian purebreds are born today, caliber horses, pure and profound. There are almost three hundred in all. Every landowner has one, perhaps two or three. He has nothing but love for them; he will be their protector and sing his most heartfelt praise. What is his dream? To have his "drinker of the wind" run in official races. And to see him win! It is a dream that comes true for the lucky and dedicated few.

Here a trainer is part of the family, a son, cousin, or uncle. And so is the jockey, who rides the horses every morning as

soon as day breaks. He gallops on a trail that he cuts through the fields and between the olive trees. In order to participate in official races, the owner has to transport the horse by truck, even though it represents a tremendous cost. Certainly, it would be less expensive to entrust the future star to a trainer in the northern region. But the people of the southern region know that, in the long run, living in the racing stable would mean losing the very qualities that distinguish their horses.

An ancient custom was recently revived along the Saharan horizon: the long-distance race. This endurance test sprang up again in Europe, the United States, Australia, and Asia some twenty years ago; it may even be introduced in the 2008 Olympic Games! It is gaining popularity everywhere and is a potential source of new glory for purebred Arabians. For it is the Asian Horse, "the lord of the air," the "drinker of the wind," that always wins.

Tunisia, a major participant in the world cup of horse racing in 1998 in Dubai, is on its way to forming its own national team. Its champion is a stallion from Maknassi named Safouen, a thirteen-year-old purebred with a silky and golden coat. His muscles are slender and lean. His eyes shine like the moon in a pitch-black night. After the race, his nostrils still trembling, he lowers his neck, kneels, and slowly rolls in the hot sand. Then he snorts and smiles as only a horse from the Sahara can.

The Inhabitants of the Pampa

ARGENTINA

In the heart of the immense Argentinian steppes, the horse is
more than an international polo star. He is man's brother,
his double: without him, the gaucho could not exist.

Equestrian games and competitions, such as horse racing and harness racing, stem from ritual war practices, hunting traditions, or livestock management. During antiquity, chariot racing took place on open and uneven ground first, and then in arenas. Rome invented bloody battles between cavaliers and every imaginable animal: bears, bulls, elephants, boars, lions, cheetahs, which were fought with a lance or bare hands. For centuries, these combats made the Roman sky resound with the extraordinary roar of joy.

During the Middle Ages in Europe, the first tournaments sometimes brought more than two thousand cavaliers face to face. But ladies of the court preferred one-on-one contests in which cavaliers wearing their colors fought with each other. After establishing a genuine tournament code, the jouster became a professional fighter who traveled from castle to castle to capitalize on his art and courage. But the death in Issa of Henry II, king of France, sounded the death knell for an impassioned game that had killed as many riders as horses in five hundred years.

The horsemen of Louis XIV's century enjoyed head and ring races, which involved toppling a kind of dummy or slipping rings into a stick. Meanwhile, on the high Pamir Plateau, on the border of China and Kashmir, *buzkashi* was played. This was an extremely brutal game in which a rider tried to catch a strangled sheep and bring it to a specific point despite the violent attacks of his adversaries—all blows were permitted. The rules have remained practically the same in Afghanistan, where *buskashi* is practiced to this day. It is undoubtedly one of the oldest equestrian games in the world, along with polo.

In fact, polo, under a different name, was first an ancient Persian sport that dates back more than two thousand years. It was given its name in Tibet, coming from the Tibetan *pulu*, meaning "ball." But it was in India that the English discovered it in 1854,

Little criollo horse, with a short gallop, long breath, loyal instinct;
little criollo horse that was like the pole for the flag he carried on his back.

BELISARIO ROLDÁN
Citation from the book *Caballos de América*
(Horses of America), by Angel Cabrera, 1945

in the state of Manipur, near Assam, where every village then had its own team and horses; the Manipur ponies measured barely 12 hands. The British planters, the merchants, the trading posts, and the officers of the Bengal army were all great fans of the game.

The first polo tournament took place in England in 1869. Hurlingham Polo Association was established as headquarters for the sport. In a few years, polo won over all of Europe, and then the United States. But the greatest rivals emerged in Argentina, where the English had formed a large community among the landowners and breeders. It should be noted that they had a large resource of well-suited horses: the Criollo horses (meaning of Spanish origin).

Indeed, after the arrival of the first Spanish colonists in 1536, horses populated the immense Argentinian Pampa

faster than men. Through their work with cattle, the horses developed the qualities required for polo: the capacity for rapid acceleration, instantaneous turning, and quick transitions, and the ability to remain calm in action and balanced while the rider is moving.

Since the end of the First World War, Argentina has been the number-one polo country in the world. There are three times as many members there as in the United States, and ten times more than in England. Among the best players, many have joined foreign teams; by virtue of which the team with the most Argentinian players in an international tournament, is the favorite team. But the true star of polo is the heir of the illustrious little Criollo, the horse that "springs between the legs of his rider." It is a horse that is raised on the slick grass of the Pampa, the land of the gaucho.

Despite the major changes brought about by modern times, the gaucho perpetuates his equestrian techniques, keeping them intact. With his science for land, and even more because of his bravery and contempt of danger, the gaucho became the very cherished livestock keeper for the estancerios. Maté, the national infusion prepared from an energizing plant, continues to be his favorite drink.

The land of the Pampa is harsh. The grass is orange, silver, brown, golden, sometimes gray, never green. There is not one tree, not even a stone; only some bushes and the discreet shimmer of dwindling water, exhausted by the battle of a horizontal crawl. It is a land without landmarks, crisscrossed with barbed wire into the distance. It is a lonely land, with barely one inhabitant per square kilometer. The Argentinian steppe forms a world that stretches from the tropics to the ice of Cape Horn, extending over thousands of miles, reaching all the way to the Andes Mountains. Winters here are polar and summers are so scorching that it is said that in Buenos Aires twelve million inhabitants "attempt" to survive until autumn.

In the heart of Patagonia, which is populated by sheep, even the grass cries against the wind, a wind that almost never lets up. Today, the wind went into its hideaway, somewhere in the southwest. Thirty-five million sheep, their coats textured like curdled milk, have gone back to grazing on the hard grass, which grows in ruffled tufts and wears down their teeth at a young age. Their horizon is defined by the gaucho, the man who has lived through the centuries without ever—or hardly ever—dismounting from his horse. But the gaucho is no longer the vagabond of yesteryear, the absolute nomad, the outlaw, the smuggler, half-caste, the fruit of one-time and often brutal love. Henceforth, he obeys one master, the *estanciero*, the owner of several thousand acres of pastures, and offers his services in return for pay.

It was barely a hundred years ago that the number of horses and livestock in the immense plain was so great that the herds belonged to anyone who made the effort to capture or hunt them. Only tongue and a few choice cuts were taken from cattle since their meat was rather tough. Cattle were worth only the price of their hide, which was used to make clothing, harnesses, seats, and bags. At the time, the gaucho was the master of the Pampa, along with the Indians, who were sometimes friends, sometimes enemies. But at the end of the nineteenth century, everything changed. With refrigeration and barbed wire fencing, meat could be exported. The Pampa, transformed into the kingdom of large landowners, was considered a rural annex of industrial Europe.

With his knowledge of land and animals and his riding skills, and even more for his bravery and contempt for danger, the gaucho became the cherished livestock keeper for the big breeding farms. But he was very often charged with the most difficult tasks, those that discouraged the *estancia's* permanent workers.

It is the beginning of summer. Beyond the Rio Negro, the Santa Rosita *estancia* is getting ready for the tremendous annual job of shearing the sheep. Don Ricardo, the owner of the property, usually lives in Buenos Aires, the young and giant capital, which was once timid and bourgeois. The city gave rise to the glossy moustache and polished shoes, which Europe had celebrated during the Jazz Age. Land and livestock still belong to the urban man—Argentina has not undergone an agrarian revolution.

Don Ricardo owns a private plane. But he only comes to Santa Rosita in the summer, the main season of gaucho activ-

My glory is to live free
Like the bird in the sky.
I build not one nest on this earth
Where there is so much suffering.
And no one must follow me
When I take flight again.

JOSÉ HERNANDEZ
Argentinian poet (1834–1886)
Excerpt from the book *Martín Fierro*,
the saga of the Pampa and the gauchos

During the summer, the gauchos
gather the sheep that graze the
lands of the estancia *by the*
thousands. In a few weeks, all
the animals will be branded,
vaccinated, and then castrated
before being sheared.

ity when sheep are gathered, sheared, vaccinated, divided, castrated, and branded. The wool is then sold and the sheep are brought to slaughter. In winter, there is nothing to do but maintain the fields and skin the dead animals. Indeed, depending on how harsh the climate is and how violent the storms are, one to ten percent of the sheep die from the cold. In Patagonia, the farmers don't use fertilizer; they don't cut the grass or feed the livestock, and they don't milk. There are only horse stables and a barn for the ram breeding.

The weeks that promise to be frantic belong to the gauchos. They will cross the wild steppes like masters, fighting to bring together some twenty thousand sheep scattered across the vast fields to lead them toward the shearing blades. Pablo Arauz is among them. All he brings with him is a *recado* (sheep skin and leather saddle), a poncho, and a *facón*, his famous all-purpose knife.

Even before the day breaks, Pablo and his eight companions are at work, carefully grooming all five horses. The five, fierce-eyed Criollos form his *tropilla*, which is led by the *madrina*, a mare wearing a bell. With such a team, he will be able to change horses as often as necessary, for it will be a long and exhausting journey. They will be tormented by the dust that will fly up as the animals walk, enveloping both man and horse, seeping into their mouths, noses, and eyes, unless rain, warm but torrential, forms immense and changing lagoons.

For this kind of voyage, the "judas" leads the way. This is the sheep that is supposed to lead in all the others. The gauchos spread out along the ends of the herd, galloping after the recalcitrant animals to push them, whistling and encouraging. They break once during the day to grill the *asado* and distribute the *maté*—the national infusion prepared from an energizing plant. The journey continues until night. It is then that everyone lays down his *recado*, covers it with his poncho, and sleeps beneath the stars with his horses. Pablo is a happy man.

The gauchos who live in this part of the world justify their name more than ever: in Quechua, one of the main Indian languages of Argentina, *huacho* means "orphan." Much is said about them; they are talked about often, as *paisanos* or *peones*, but few, in fact, know them. They belong to another world and are forced to be strict with themselves because their milieu is hostile toward them. Isolated and hardened,

The gaucho's boots used to be made from colt hide. Today, they are patent leather and pleated. They still have elaborate spurs called espuelas.

The traditional bombachas, or baggy pants, continue to be worn, just like the "coin-purse" belt, inlaid with money or medallions, in which the gaucho keeps his facón, his knife with finely wrought handle.

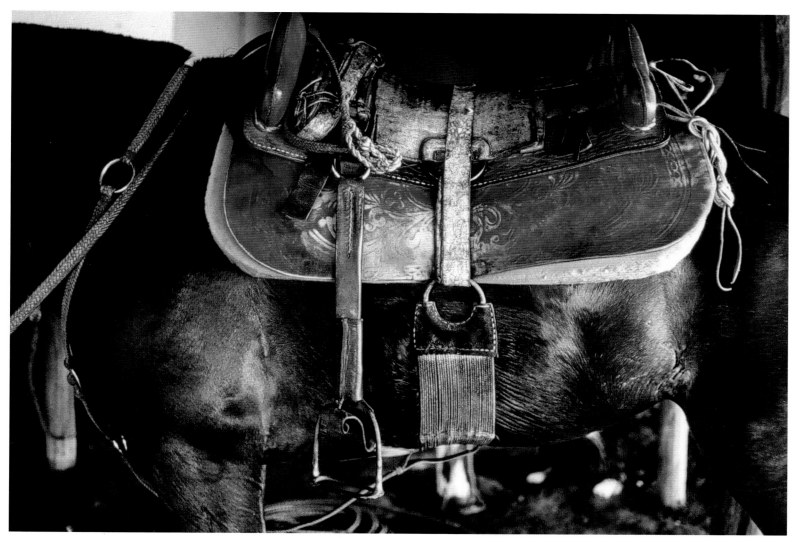

By living in the wild and in herds, the criollos can face any challenge. When young horses are broken in, there is a genuine show, with a banquet, a dance, and traditional songs.

He fled, leaving all behind;
Forever poor and hunted,
He wanders like a damned soul
Without a nest, as if he had no lair,
To be gaucho, sapristi;
That, surely, is a crime.

AN ANONYMOUS ESTANCIERO

they count only on themselves and their horses. Being a gaucho is a way of life, a frame of mind.

When he is at a *puesto*, one of the isolated posts in the middle of the Pampa where the gauchos spend more than six months watching over the fields and the animals, Pablo sleeps on the ground; but his horses have bedding so that they can rest as comfortably as possible. He chose them himself, then captured them in the Pampa, in accordance with standards, that haven't changed in three centuries: endurance, courage, spirit, resistance. Then he blindfolded their eyes to tame them. This is an ancestral, brutal method, but it is fast and effective. Here a horse that is ill suited for the keeper's hard work is sold, perhaps even slaughtered. The mutual dependence between man and horse is complete, danger is everywhere, and the slightest fall can have serious consequences. The holes dug by the armadillos are fatal traps for horses.

During the seasonal migration, if the gauchos come across a herd of wild Criollos, they will be able to point out immediately from afar which ones they want. But the *estanciero* will be the one to decide which ones to capture. The "Criollo hunt" and taming takes the gaucho back to his roots, something that thrills him. On this occasion, the *domador*, the official horsebreaker of the *estancia*, calls to them. And everyone wants to participate. They choose the most stubborn horses to break in as a matter of pride. It is a true spectacle to which city people are invited. The Argentines are captivated by this kind of rodeo. Although this is a modern country that doesn't shy away from progress, city dwellers are set on preserving the image of the gaucho, the symbol the country.

When they ardently fought for their country's independence, the gauchos wrote one of the most important pages in Argentinian history. But their disdain for law and their love of freedom never pleased authorities, who, as early as the end of the eighteenth century, were determined to bring the nomad to heel. They already had a reputation of being smugglers and animal thieves. Vagrancy was therefore proclaimed a crime, and anyone living in the Pampa was forced to carry work papers, which were to be regularly checked by a boss. Threatened by mandatory draft into the army, the gaucho had to comply. Today, his wandering is limited. He can only change bosses if he tires of a place. And yet he is a gaucho and will remain a gaucho. On Sundays,

His home is the Pampa;
His den is the desert,
And if, starving for food,
He attacks a colt
The others will chase him
And accuse him of being a thief.

JOSÉ HERNANDEZ

this lone rider goes to the *pulpería*, a kind of rural bar near the track. Here, he gambles. He loves all games: cock fighting, cards, horse racing. He is capable of betting his whole salary away down to the last peso! Sometimes, he will pick up a guitar and sing about the good old days when his ancestors would capture wild bulls with the *boleadora*—a hunting weapon borrowed from the Indians made of three straps and filled with stones. If it were thrown correctly, it would wrap around the animal's feet. But playing *pato* brings the most pleasure.

Originating in the Pampa more than three hundred years ago, the game of *pato* was forbidden for a long time because it was so brutal: the gauchos would fight over a living duck all the way to the *estancia* at a gallop, spurring on the fowl with lasso and knife. But it has been revived over the past couple of years, due to a handful of enthusiastic defenders of Argentinian equestrian tradition. Today, it is a team sport; a real sport with a ball equipped with handles and a clearly marked field. The game is divided into six chukkers, like in polo. The rider has a different horse every chukker. An open tournament takes place in Buenos Aires every year. *Pato* has found its fans, who are avid and come to celebrate the gauchos, who carry the dreams of magnitude and freedom for an entire people.

The World of the Trotter

FRANCE

There are ten thousand races every year in France, with
five million fans, and champion horses. The trotting race
hasn't lost any of its popular rural nature in the
two hundred years since it emerged in Normandy.

History

Barely domesticated, horses quickly proved to be strong and obedient. Prehistoric men used them with oxen and sometimes donkeys to pull plows or other farming implements. But harnessing techniques did not really develop until the first major urban civilizations of the Near East.

The first chariot dates back to Ur, one of the principal Sumerian cities. It was very heavy, with four solid wheels, and was used first for transportation, then for religious ceremonies. The light war chariot emerged a thousand years later, probably on the high Anatolian plateaus. It had two wheels with spokes and was pulled by two horses. Various armies from Central Asia to the Sahara used the chariot for centuries; it was also used for hunting and became an exciting vehicle for sports!

In Greece, even before the first Olympic games, chariot races were widespread and the winners received considerable prizes. The Romans, who carried on this tradition, built monumental amphitheaters. In the stands of Circus Maximus, there was room for 385,000 spectators, and twenty-four races all took place here during one day. Up to ten horses were harnessed to the chariots, which were built lighter and lighter so that only a slender two-wheeled trestle with a shield would protect the driver's knees.

During Roman times, horses were first used as entertainment for lords, then for professional sport, one that was dangerous and risky, but had big returns. The horses belonged to large organizations that adopted the colors of their coach drivers: the Blues, the Reds, the Whites, etc. Colors have remained the symbol of racing stables to this day. The Roman Empire never used horses to their fullest potential on the battlefield, so the use of the chariot gradually became obsolete and the great Roman ways crumbled.

The vehicles of the late Middle Ages were rare and heavy, even more primitive than those advanced by the Gauls. The great irony of history is that agriculture and transportation settled on the ox,

When they trotted through the wheat fields, they ran on the ears, without bending them; when they trotted on the wide ocean back, they ran on the crest of breakers of the whitening sea.

EXCERPT FROM *The Iliad*, CANTO XX

while clergy chose the donkey and mule. Horse breeding and trade were in fact reserved for the police and nobility. It was not until the eighteenth century that the horse could be found among peasant classes.

In the face of the growing needs of the transportation and war industry, western Europe produced more and more draft horses and established more breeds; for example, the Percheron in France, the Norfolk Roadster in England, or the Rhenish drafthorse in Germany. Harnessing and coaches grew in variety and were perfected. Both in the United States and Russia, trotter breeds—the Standardbred and the Orlov—were already being bred for great racetrack speed. Although the French cavalry suffered a lack of horses during the Second Empire, a horse meant to be harnessed and ridden was being bred in Normandy, where remarkable coach builders emerged.

It was to be the Anglo-Norman horse. The future manager of National Stud Farm, Ephrem Honel, set out to perfect the breed through competition. The first trotting race, improvised on the beach of Cherbourg in 1836, marked the beginning of a trotting era in France.

In less than a century, the world of harness racing, which until that point had revolved around Norfolk Roadsters, was regulated by a society that wrote and applied racing codes to trotting, and that built several racetracks and established a solid program. Henceforth, breeders would ardently fight for the French trotter so that it could rival the American Standardbred. Today, 10,000 races take place every year in France, mainly outside of Paris, and are cheered on by millions of fans and devout race goers. But it is in Paris—in Vincennes to be precise—that the fate of trotting is played out.

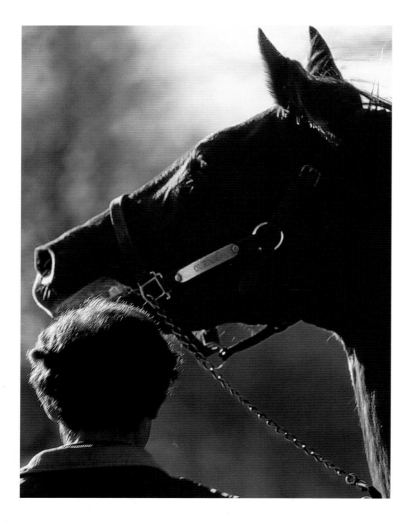

With his personality, and fifty-eight victories, Ourasi, the four-time winner of the Prix d'Amérique, will forever be the unbeatable champion of the twentieth century.

RIGHT: *Far from the racetracks and crowds, the beaches of Normandy, made smooth by the tide, offer the most beautiful, the largest, and the best trails for training in the world.*

The Vincennes racetrack is ready to burst. Thirty thousand fans have their eyes fixed on a row of breasts streaked with lather and upright necks ready to go in the starting gate. Everyone tries to find his horse. Hopes are high during this 1990 Prix d'Amerique. "And they're off! Ourasi pulls ahead on the outside. On the inside, Reine du Corta and Potin d'Amour. Reine du Corta falls back! . . . Poussy Cat from Vendée moves through and takes the lead. The home stretch, Ourasi in the lead next to Poussy Cat. Potin d'Amour and Poronto are at their tails. Poussy Cat is gaining on him. Potin d'Amour hangs on. But Ourasi pulls away! He's flying! Home stretch . . . Twenty yards before the finish line. Ourasi is a length and a half behind Potin d'Amour. Go handsome prince! Go! Go! Yes! Ourasi has crossed the finish line. 3'19"3. He has broken the record." The announcers, the fans, journalists, and trotting fanatics all chant "Ourasi" in unison, the "trotter of the century," the "extraterrestrial," the "genius," who has just won the most important race in the world for the fourth time. Unheard of!

Indolent during training, irascible in his stall, and unbeatable on the track, the cherished child of Jean-René Gougeon, his driver-trainer, has ruled over French trotting for more than five years. What is Ourasi's average trotting speed? About 25 miles per hour. When he picks up his pace, he can go almost 30 miles per hour—which is how fast a

In winter, the talent trots … at the speed of light.
Ancient and fantastic aurora borealis, the trotter
is in the ring in wind and cold.

VINCENT LEROY
Horse journalist

Thoroughbred gallops. With his personality and talent, Ourasi, who holds the world record in earnings, will forever be the unbeatable champion of the twentieth century. Today he is happily retired in Normandy, where he was born.

In the trotting world, everyone—owner, trainer, driver, or all three at once—has thought about one day participating in the Prix d'Amérique. It is the best trotting race in the world. It's a classic 2,700-meter race, one of the two largest trotting races in Europe, along with Elitloppet at the Solvalla racecourse in Sweden. The myth of this race, in which small stables have no qualms about facing big ones, has hypnotized generations of athletes since 1920. They all dream of joining the list of legendary names: Uranie, Gélinotte, Jamin, Roquépine, Bellino II, Idéal du Gazeau, Ourasi, Varenne, and others.

Princes. Yes, princes. They are all too graceful, too strong, and filled with the fever of winning; there is such extreme harmony with nature and some of its mysteries. We cannot wonder too much about them. The trotting horses are princes. They are born in the richest stud farms and in the most humble farmhouses. Sometimes they hide behind yearlings no one wants, bought for pennies, only to have the whole world staring at them a few years later. Often, an individual man or woman who believes in them will make the difference. The example of Ourasi is not uncommon: born in Saint-Étienne-l'Allier at the home of Raoul Ostheimer, who was then a breeder, trainer, and driver with American roots, the "trotter of the twentieth century" was the lovechild of Greyhound, an unknown stallion at the time, and a modest broodmare named Fleurasie.

Often trained by a driver who is also his stable boy and owner, the trotter belongs to a single man. Race after race, the couple tell a story of love and passion.

It is true that fate is sometimes sealed before birth, through parents—the more a stallion and brood mare have succeeded in racing, the greater their chances are of producing offspring like themselves. This is the breeder's science; he is a genuine alchemist of blood, an architect of genealogies who, daydreams of a world filled with home stretches and finishing lines, aspires to a wise coupling that will produce a champion. But every now and then, chance plays a role. Today in France, fifteen thousand breeders can dream of creating a Prix d'Amérique winner! The big names, horses and owners combined, rely on Normandy, the birthplace of the trotter and his saga.

Hills topped by fleecy clouds, fields with cows, apple trees, warm air filled with a salty smell and the fragrance of flowers. . . . Normandy is the very image of serenity. A region that faces the sea, its hedged farmland is its secret, a landscape of whispering small towns, half-timbered houses, and barren roads bordered by a tunnel of hedges. Everywhere, the grass is a fresh sea green, dotted with English ray-grass and white clovers. Fourteen hundred horse breeders share

You cannot train a horse with shouts and expect it to obey a whisper.

DAGOBERT D. RUNES
Letters to My Son

FOLLOWING SPREAD: *Only large stables have the option of giving their athletes to a trainer at Grosbois, the prestigious horse center that houses some fifteen hundred trotters. It is the real training ground for Paris-Vincennes.*

the single department of Calvados. Some three thousand foals are born here every year, half of which are trotters destined for the races.

In the first days of fall, a light rain moistens the farmland, which becomes a blurry world for fairies and goblins. Free in their pastures, mares and foals delight in fine grasses, unconcerned about their destiny. Indeed, as early as their seventh month, the foals will be weaned and brought to a smaller field or an individual stall. There they are exposed to a number of people, which eases their first days of training.

The spirit of competition did not suddenly come to Normandy like a wind from the sea. It came gradually, starting in 1830, to the peasants who used horses for agricultural work. In a period when the military was in search of sturdy but fast horses, the people of Normandy provided a new equine race: the Anglo-Norman.

The first trotting races founded by Ephrem Honel, who then directed the National Stud Farm, charmed the Norman breeders. Soon, the beaches could no longer accommodate

these new racing events. Racetracks were built in Cherbourg, Dieppe, Saint-Lô, Alençon, Avranches, Rouen, Falaises, and elsewhere. The Society for the Improvement of French Trotters was established on October 21, 1864. It wrote the regulations for trotting races and, through its commissioners, supervised their strict application throughout the country.

In Paris, however, which was then a bastion for the English Thoroughbred, the emergence of a nonroyal horse was met with some disdain. It was not until September 7, 1879, that trotting finally found a home in the capital. After a hard-fought struggle, the French trotter won acclaim and the hearts of sportsmen. The Gravelles plateau in Vincennes was from this point on devoted to trotting, both under saddle and in harness, and would become the "temple of trotting." The center in Grosbois became its training ground.

Yet most races take places outside of Paris: 260 racetracks, more than 9,000 races per year, more than 13,000 runners . . . The Paris Mutuel Urbain totals almost fifteen billion francs (approximately 2 billion dollars)! Small bets make up the top end of the market for many trainers. French trotting has clearly retained the traits of its rural and popular origins even though the trotter often belongs to a single man, who is owner, driver, and jockey all at once. "It's a very hard job to have today . . . but our passion for competition is what keeps us going, and we're driven by a dream: each horse could be a potential champion," says Hervé Bihel, who founded his training center in Saint-Gatien-des-Bois, the Norman hamlet in which he settled many years ago. Twenty-five trotters are carefully tended in their half-timbered stables, and the work is intensive. Half of them race and the others are young horses in training. They don't take any days off, not even a Sunday. Every day the horses are fed their portion of grain as early as six in the morning. The first horse comes out at seven, harnessed to a sulky. As part of their routine, they are jogged around the sand track so that they stretch their legs and get their breathing and muscles going.

Hervé Bihel, like most of the trainer-drivers, first chose this profession because of the sport and the pleasure. Then he learned to believe in the virtues of patience and work, as well as humility, which, is often the best attitude with a horse. Out of the fifteen colts he breaks in at any given time,

It's often wheel-to-wheel in these races, and the average speed is forty-six kilometers per hour. Each horse has its own way of making it to the head of the pack. A sprinter can attain ninety-six kilometers an hour, which is how fast a thoroughbred gallops.

Breed the best to the best and hope for the best.

TRADITIONAL BREEDING ADVICE

only seven will see a racetrack, perhaps two will earn their keep. What about the star horse or at least the high-level athlete that appears unexpectedly one day, elevating the stud farm to the top? Hervé Bihel can dream about it, but it would be a rare occurrence.

At about eighteen months the young trotter begins his training. In only a few days, the horse learns to walk on a lunge line and then to tolerate a girth. The horse is then harnessed to a "trainer," a kind of heavy sulky, before he meets the classic sulky. Now starts the real work: gait adjustment, breath and muscle conditioning. This is a crucial step for the trainer who can detect the true qualities of his young

recruits and let go of horses without a future—the horses who have a "bad heart," as they say in horse racing jargon. Indeed, the door to the racetrack is hard to get through. In trotting, there is a "qualification" test that young horses have to take before a judge. The distance and time are determined according to age. Only a qualified trotter can run in the races.

As opposed to a flat racer, which is retired soon after its first triumphant victories in the world's greatest races, the career of a big trotter is often much longer. In France, the horse can not run past the age of ten, but abroad, especially in Switzerland, Belgium, and Malta, it can race until it's fifteen or sixteen years old. The trainer tries to do all he can to keep up the horse mentally and physically, rather than encourage its speed. And the farm worker, wearing his blue uniform and boots, relies on long trots down the huge beaches to keep up the horse's morale.

The driver has to have a light touch and listen to his horse. From his sulky, he can only communicate with his horse by hand and voice. The reins also force the trotter to hold its head high, which keeps him from "falling" into a gallop.

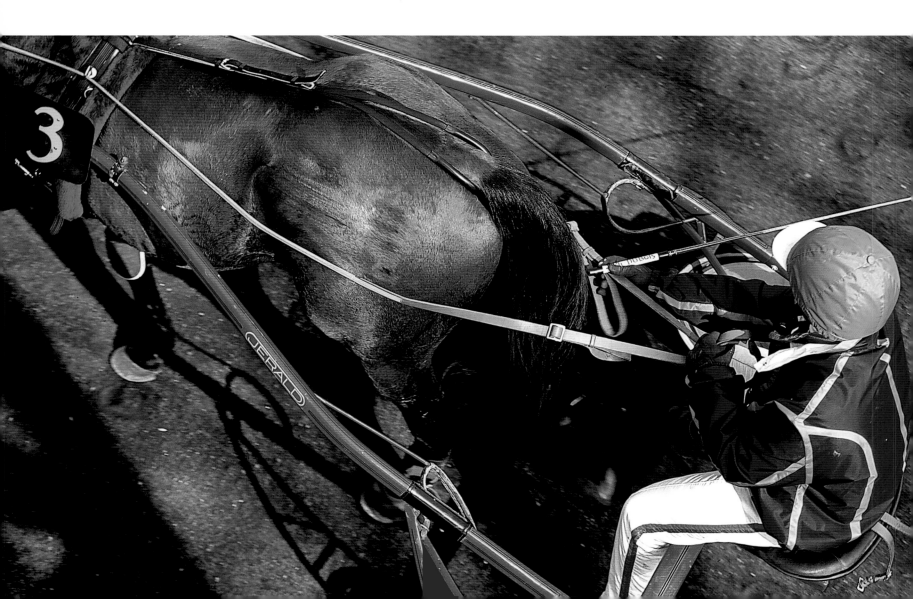

So today, the sea is in charge of the horse's first training. The receding tide uncovers the most beautiful, and best trails in the world. The air is invigorating, the seagulls cry as they skim the waves of an iridescent ocean that crashes and foams against the beach.

There are no footpaths, no sounds, just the muffled vibration of the sulky wheels and the quiet pounding of hoofs on the wet sand. Upon the order of Hervé Bihel, who stands serenely on his sulky, Hermès le Fol sets out on a lively, airy, and suspended trot. The wind coming in off the ocean fills the heart and lungs of this six-year-old trotter with joy. He is diligent, powerful, superb. The sun shines golden, orange, and yellow off of his coat. On New Year's Day 2001, they won their first victory together in Vincennes. What is this princely trotter's destiny? Certainly he will always give his all. But the future is unknown, and his chances remain a mystery.

Its pupils bursting from the flash of cameras, its sides sucked with fright, its ears flat because of an excited crowd that has exploded, the compact group tears down the track before the stands and throws itself, chest first, down to the stables.

HOMÉRIC
French writer (born in 1954), former French jockey, then a horse journalist for *Libération*; citation taken from the book *Ourasi: Le Roi Fainéant*, 1989

Step by Step in the Andes

SOUTH AMERICA

For an inhabitant of the Andes, horses are inseparable companions in
work and travel. During village festivities and ferias, horses are heroes.
Elegant parades are organized to show them off. The horse is the
caballo de paso, the sun child, the son of the wind.

The only way for a human being to move is to put one foot in front of the other. But, with its four legs, the horse has more options. According to studies of horse locomotion, conducted by a team of researchers at the University of Zurich, the horse has some fifty-five different gaits. Only four among them are said to be natural: walking, trotting, pacing, and galloping. Jumping and reining-back can be added to the list. Some specialists only recognize two: the walk, used for long distances, and the gallop, used when trying to escape. But according to the criteria of classical riding, the pace is an irregular gait, flawed, even artificial. La Guérinière talked about it in this way: "you have to distinguish the perfect gaits—walking, trotting, galloping—from the flawed ones—pacing, the rack, the amble. The former come purely from nature and were never perfected by Art. And the latter stem from a weak and ruined na-

ture." A general survey nevertheless points to a different viewpoint.

Ancient history very often refers to pacing horses, or gaited horses, and their range of movement. They can be recognized in Etruscan frescoes, in Chinese sculpture from the Han Dynasty, and in images of Egyptian and Roman chariots. The Middle Ages produced the saddle horse par excellence, or palfreys, as opposed to the steed, the warhorse selected for its manageability on the battlefield. Women rode almost exclusively "laterally gaited horses."

Until the sixteenth century, the trotter was considered a warhorse, the poor man's horse or a pack or draft horse. But in the following century, the situation changed dramatically: gaited horses disappeared from the equestrian scene. A hundred years later, Europe had forgotten them. The first reason for this disfavor was the emergence of classical dressage. Indeed, the exercises the knights performed as they prepared for battle were trotting and cantering. The development of galloping races also explains why pacing horses were overlooked.

But pacing horses did not disappear! Icelandic ponies, which had been living on their island for a thousand years, retained the genetic capacity to produce a lateral gait. In South America, the Colombian, Peruvian, and Puerto Rican Pasos, the Argentinian Criollo, the Brazilian Campolino and Magalarga are laterally gaited horses descended from the Spanish horses brought by the conquistadors in the sixteenth century. In North America, the descendants of the hobbies and palfreys from Europe, are the source of the American Saddlebred, the Tennessee Walker, and the Standardbred.

There are many other kinds of gaited horses in the world, particularly in Asia and Africa, where riding is not only for the elite. The ambling Abyssinian mule, the South African basuto pony, the Chinese pacer, the pony of Altai or Bashir: all have left their genetic mark on modern horses, even if it is difficult to talk about "breeds," for standards have never been clearly defined. In Europe, finally, the development of horseback riding gradually brought back pacing horses from their distant past. Indeed, they didn't lose their raison d'être: comfort in a saddle. More and more appreciated by foreign riders, they have also benefited from new ways of thinking in the horse world, which is well illustrated by the growing success of American equitation.

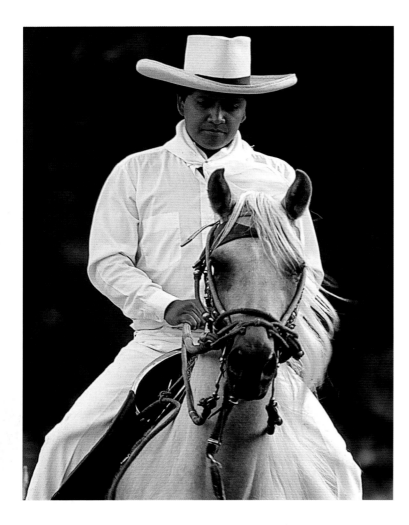

Distant relatives of the horses of the Conquest, the pasos live in the wild, in all kinds of weather. They are sturdy and, besides walk, trot, and gallop, can amble in a particularly fast manner that is comfortable for the rider. It is a natural gait that South American breeders have been able to preserve through rigorous selection.

They are perhaps the most impressive mountains in the world. More than 3,500 miles of massive walls, steep rock faces, jagged, craggy, carved peaks, with cliff roads resting against emptiness, glaciers, lakes and deserts balanced on top of sharp ridges, and volcanic cones rising against a pale blue sky, whipped by ocean winds. The Andes mountain range rises in Colombia, passes through Ecuador, stretches across all of Chile, culminates in Argentina, and dies at Cape Horn. It is the spinal cord of South America. To man, and to other mountains in the world, the Andes are a big lesson in humility.

Seized with anxiety, a feeling of being crushed, of being truly isolated, the people of the Andes nevertheless do not feel small. Quite the opposite. They have waged an unsuspected war since the beginning of time. The Incas, who used llamas for transportation, marked trails, crossed gorges, scaled steep rock faces. Royal roads crossed their empire from Colombia to the center of Chile, roads that the conquistadors transformed into brutal and bloody routes. The three centuries of colonization only benefited trade between the fertile valleys and the rest of the continent. Then, from the time of independence to the present, major civil engineering projects focused on developing a network of paths and roads that allow highland peasants to come down into the market towns. But, in this frenzied land, the hamlets and the villages, which are only a few miles apart as the crow flies, are always separated by long, exhausting journeys by foot, punctuated by peaks and valleys.

Many countries draw on the assets of Spain...
Why are they so valuable, we do not know: no one
has mentioned the fine horses yet; such horses have
not been seen anywhere else in the world.

FERNÁN GONZÁLEZ
Excerpt from *Caballos de América,*
by Angel Cabrera, 1945

Because they undergo selective
breeding and are kept pure, the
paso fino *are docile but lively.*
They have great talent and very
supple gaits.

For these anonymous lives which throb in the shadows of the valleys, the horse introduced by the conquistadors has remained an inseparable companion for work and travel. Nature and time have made the horse into a hardy, small-sized animal. Its step is confident, and its resistance is truly extraordinary. The horse is persistent and hardworking. And the Andes people have sought out the smoothest gaits for it: the lateral gaits, which stem from the amble. This is the *caballo de paso*, or Paso Fino, the sun child, the son of the wind.

Suppleness, power, will, generosity: the Paso Fino has it all. The horse's experience lies in the long journeys walking through the intimidating rocky mountains, through the deceiving stretches of land of the plateaus and plains, over the salt and sand cracking under its little ambling steps. On market day in town, the horse can be found on the central square, waiting for its master with resignation. Its muscled back and croup, strong and sturdy, its solid legs, with short cannon bones and hard feet, are highly valued. The unusual coat is admired. The brown *zaíno* with black mane, the *moro* that is a bluish gray, the peach-colored *risillo*, the white speckled *tordillo*, the *oscuro* as black as coal . . . Despite it's small size, the Paso Fino is considered to be very elegant.

Wherever horses are relegated to leisure and sports, the ideal model is large in size. Breeders are now producing giants built like tanks, capable of jumping ever higher, running ever faster on the racetrack! But what's the use of having long legs when steep paths require small steps? Aren't low and ambling gaits, which are so comfortable for riders,

A horse is a thing of beauty …
none will tire of looking at him as long
as he displays himself in his splendor.

XENOPHON
On Horsemanship

essential when transporting merchandise or livestock for a full day? Latin Americans understand this well. They have developed breeds of horses that are so original; today they are recognized as a race in itself. Over the past decades, in Colombia, Puerto Rico, and Peru, the Paso Fino has become the hero of village festivities and ferias. Conformation and performance competitions are devoted to them.

The celebration starts with the *cabalgata*, a colorful and dynamic parade. It is a strange combination of swaying, of radiant eyes, crimson nostrils, arched backs, and the sound of horseshoes. Hundreds of riders, sometimes thousands, parade through the streets and avenues, dancing spectacularly as they take their small steps. Indeed, for Latin Americans, dance is second nature. And dance means music. And music, moreover, seems to have cult status. There is not one street corner, not one café terrace, house, bus, or taxi where music cannot be heard. It is the voice of a people who sing of their joys and pains, who tell their stories and speak of their passions. In this part of the world, man and horse have been in a relationship that has spanned five centuries and they have written a special music together. The harmony between rider and horse, moving together, sometimes gives rise to strange ballets.

On the day of the feria in Monteria, in Colombia, hooves shine everywhere. In front of the fairground stables, the Paso Finos get ready for the final gait competition. With eyes bulging, necks rising above their glossy chests, with saliva on their lips, they fly beneath their riders in the orange light of a rising sun. Five thousand fans await them

Blessed are the horses and blessed are the living
that had to live in the savanna of Bogotá.

J.M. MARROQUÍN
Excerpt from *Caballos de América*,
by Angel Cabrera, 1945

in the *coliseo*, the large theatre: Ten thousand square meters of sand topped by a resonant floor—the floor for dancing horses. It's a full house.

The fairgrounds are thick with people and the stables are surrounded by curious crowds who take in the Paso Fino with their eyes or cameras. The riders wear ceremonial costumes, the *vaqueros* in jeans, sporting shirt fronts and black glasses; others, more traditional, wear a vest, hat, and *ruana* on their shoulders; there are many children dressed like their elders, women dressed to the nines, mothers squeezing their children's hand, groups of young girls and flirting teenagers. . . . And, above the din of the crowd, the cacophony of music rises from the open-air dance halls.

The *coliseo* loudspeakers announce the opening of the ball. The moment has arrived. The jury takes it place in the seats of honor, and the crowd packs the stands. The music stops all of a sudden. There is only the muffled sound of words, laughter, and whispers. Twelve contestants emerge onto the light sand. They take small, nervous, and buoyant steps that beat softly.

Riders wear a *chaquetilla* (short jacket) over cuffed pants, *zamarros* (leggings) that drag in the sand, and an *ancha* hat on their heads.

Their limbs shaking, the horses start their turn around the track, showing off. With their necks arched like rainbows, they roll their shoulders, swaying their hips. They are nervous down to their feet, which hit the ground like a tap dancer. Their long manes wave with of their steps, while the riders' movements are barely detectable. The

The horses born in Peru from the best Castilian line have become valorous and robust.

ABONDANO DE HERRERA, 1940

On market days in the village, coffee growers, peasants and livestock keepers fill the little streets. There horses wait in the village square for their masters, with age-old resignation.

steady left hand holding the reins is all that is one sees. The other hand rests softly on the rider's leg. A rogue dancer takes advantage of the serious exhibition and plays the clown. A horse bucks and is automatically eliminated. On the judge's command, the eleven remaining contestants quickly regroup in a corner of the outdoor arena, ready to compete. Their feet dance in place. Time has come for the individual competition. A roar rises from the crowd and immediately hushes.

A stallion with a soft coppery coat, shimmering with long metallic strips of the harness, steps into the center of the ring. The horse is Gracioso, ten years old, one of the day's favorites. The hammering of his hooves suddenly sounds over the loudspeaker, like a drum roll. His legs weave in all directions. But his head is steady and his back is taut like a bow. The rider's back is arched, his gaze crackles, his forehead

The horse, like cattle and cereal, has accompanied man over the entire globe, from the Ganges to Rio de la Plate, from the African coasts to the perched plateaus of Antisana that reach higher in altitude than the top of Tenerife.

ALEXANDER VON HUMBOLT
German explorer (1769–1859)
Known for his work in the American tropics and in central Asia.
Excerpt from *Caballos de América*, by Angel Cabrera, 1945

The traditional Peruvian harness accentuates the dancing gait of the Paso Fino. A leather piece highlights the specificity of the horse's tail, which is low and hangs free.

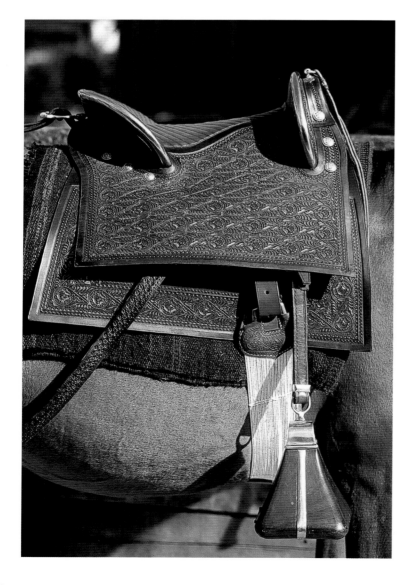

In Columbia, the beauty of the Paso Fino gaits is judged in special competitions. It is at this time that regional riders participate in the cabalgada, *a joyful and lively parade.*

is turned toward the sky, and his left hand is relaxed. The dance speaks of the nobility and sensuality of flamenco dancing. The whole crowd devours the spectacle, and the jury does the same. Everyone listens to the music of the steps, its rhythm, its cadence, its power. The steps are indeed the music of victory, even though the beauty and perfection of the dance are also essential criteria.

After each performance, the judge comments and the crowd murmurs. Then feet begin to dance again on the floor. Four, five, ten rounds are necessary to decide between the best before all the contestants are invited to leave the track. During the jury deliberations, there's a great hullabaloo: vendors push through the stands—drinks, meat skewers,

A Horse already knows how to be a horse;
the rider has to learn how to become a rider.
A horse without a rider is still a horse; a rider
without a horse is no longer a rider.

ANONYMOUS

fries, grilled corn!—shouldering impassioned aficionados, exacerbated betters.

When the time comes to name the winners, each groom brings his champion, white with foam, back into the ring, charging through the hall that leads to the *coliseo*. The riders, their souls buzzing to the sound of the shoes, get back up into their saddles, holding their proud posture. When the dancers return, the crowd applauds, roars and whistles in the *coliseo*.

It is certain that the popularity of the winners will soar. As will their value. It should not be forgotten that the Paso Fino, like the Peruvian Paso, is a luxury horse. Depending on the breeding line, model, and medals earned, an individual horse can be worth more than a million dollars. So, the horse is a real star. Treated like a king, monitored like an athlete, it leads a dream life. Its breeding life is luxurious, punctuated by a few competitions and the occasional parade. On the day that it closes its eyes, this sun child will gallop off toward the clouds that float over the Andes. The horse might even be stuffed, its memory revered in its master's living room.

Editor, English-language edition: Matthew Giles

Design Coordinator, English-language edition: Tina Thompson

Library of Congress Cataloging-in-Publication Data

Ripart, Jacqueline.

   [Chevaux du monde. English]

   Horses of the world : the wild and the tame / by Jacqueline Ripart ; translated from the French by Molly Stevens and Catherine Reep.

     p. cm.

   ISBN 0-8109-1195-7

    1.   Horses—History. I. Title.

   SF283 .R5713 2002

   636.1'009—dc21   2001055236

Printed and bound in Italy

10 9 8 7 6 5 4 3 2 1

Harry N. Abrams, Inc.

100 Fifth Avenue

New York, N.Y. 10011

www.abramsbooks.com

Abrams is a subsidiary of